# Canadian Fiction Studies

*Other volumes in preparation*

*Rachel's Children:* 48
MARGARET LAURENCE'S

*A Jest*
*of God*

*Nora Stovel*

E C W   P R E S S

Copyright © ECW PRESS, 1992

CANADIAN CATALOGUING IN PUBLICATION DATA

Stovel, Nora Foster.
Rachel's Children : Margaret Laurence's A jest of God

(Canadian fiction studies ; no. 12)
Includes bibliographical references.
Includes index.
ISBN 1–55022–126–4

1. Laurence, Margaret, 1926–1987. Jest of God.
1. Title. 11. Series.

PS8523.A86J437 1992    C813'.54    C90-094509-5
PR9199.3.L38J437 1992

This book has been published with the assistance of grants
from the Ontario Arts Council, The Canada Council, and
the Government of Canada Department of Communications.
The development of the Canadian Fiction Studies was
assisted by the Government of Ontario through
the Ministry of Culture and Communications.

The cover features a reproduction of the dust-wrapper
from the first edition of *A Jest of God*, courtesy of the
Thomas Fisher Rare Book Library, University of Toronto.
Frontispiece photograph by Boult Photographics, Mississauga,
Ontario, reproduced courtesy of David Laurence.
Design and imaging by ECW Type & Art, Oakville, Ontario.
Printed and bound by Hignell Printing, Winnipeg, Manitoba.

Distributed by General Publishing Co. Limited
30 Lesmill Road, Don Mills, Ontario M3B 2T6

Published by ECW PRESS,
1980 Queen Street East, Second Floor,
Toronto, Ontario M4L 1J2

# Table of Contents

# A Note on the Author

Nora Foster Stovel is Associate Professor of English at the University of Alberta, where she teaches modern British literature, as well as Canadian and contemporary women's fiction. She received the B.A., M.A., and Ph.D. from McGill, Cambridge, and Dalhousie Universities respectively, followed by Postdoctoral Fellowships at the University of Calgary. Nora Stovel has published numerous articles on modern British literature and contemporary Canadian and women's fiction in *ARIEL*, *The D.H. Lawrence Review*, *English Literature in Transition*, *Essays on Canadian Writing*, *English Studies in Canada*, *The International Fiction Review*, and *Mosaic*, and in D.H. Lawrence, Margaret Drabble, and Margaret Laurence *Festschriften*. She has published *Margaret Drabble: Symbolic Moralist* (1989) and is currently working on *D.H. Lawrence: From Playwright to Novelist* and *Margaret Laurence, Diviner*. She has also authored *Introducing Margaret Laurence's The Fire-Dwellers* for the Canadian Fiction Studies series and is composing *A Biography of Margaret Laurence* for ECW's Canadian Biography Series. Nora Stovel lives in Edmonton with her husband Bruce Stovel and their two children.

Rachel's Children:
Margaret Laurence's
*A Jest of God*

*For My Sister*

# Chronology

| | |
|---|---|
| 1926 | Jean Margaret Wemyss born 18 July in Neepawa, Manitoba. |
| 1944–47 | Attends United College, Winnipeg. Completes B.A. in Honours English. |
| 1947 | Works as a reporter on the *Winnipeg Citizen*. Marries Jack Laurence, a hydraulic engineer. |
| 1949 | Moves to England. |
| 1950 | Moves to Somaliland, where Jack builds dams in the desert. |
| 1952 | Moves from Somaliland to Ghana. Jocelyn born. |
| 1954 | *A Tree for Poverty*. David born. |
| 1957 | Moves from Ghana to Vancouver. |
| 1960 | *This Side Jordon*. |
| 1962 | Separates from Jack Laurence. Moves with children to Buckinghamshire, England. |
| 1963 | *The Tomorrow-Tamer, The Prophet's Camel Bell*. |
| 1964 | *The Stone Angel*. |
| 1966 | *A Jest of God*. |
| 1968 | *Long Drums and Cannons: Nigerian Dramatists and Novelists 1952–1966*. |
| 1969 | Divorced from Jack Laurence. |
| 1969 | *The Fire-Dwellers*. |
| 1970 | *A Bird in the House, Jason's Quest*. |
| 1971 | Companion of the Order of Canada. |
| 1974 | Returns to Canada and lives henceforward at Lakefield, Ontario. *The Diviners*. |
| 1975 | Receives the Molson Award. |

| 1976 | *Heart of a Stranger.* |
|------|------------------------|
| 1979 | *Six Darn Cows, The Olden Days Coat.* |
| 1981 | Appointed Chancellor of Trent University. *A Christmas Birthday Story.* |
| 1987 | Died 5 January in Lakefield, Ontario. |
| 1989 | *Dance on the Earth: A Memoir* published posthumously. |

# The Importance of the Work

A book has importance both for its writer and its readers. For Margaret Laurence herself, *A Jest of God* was an important work for several reasons. First, Laurence, who was orphaned as a young child, comes face to face in this novel with the fact of death, especially the loss of a parent — in this case the heroine's father. Death also raises the issue of Providence, for the loss of both her parents during her childhood must have caused Laurence to question the goodness of God. The title, *A Jest of God*, suggests that the subject of providence will be one of Laurence's major themes in this novel.

*A Jest of God* is one of a pair of sister novels, for Rachel Cameron, heroine of *A Jest of God* (1966), and Stacey Cameron MacAindra, the protagonist of Laurence's next novel, *The Fire-Dwellers* (1969), are sisters. Opposing personae of the author perhaps, the two sisters are opposites who have gone in very different directions: Rachel is a stereotypical spinster school teacher who still lives in her home town of Manawaka with her aging mother, whereas Stacey escaped early to marry and live in Vancouver with her salesman husband, Clifford MacAindra, and their brood of four children. For Laurence, writing these novels may have been an exercise in "the road not taken." As both novels open, the estranged sisters have not seen each other for seven years, but by the end of each novel, they will be en route to reunion. But first, each sister must learn to empathize with the other in order to develop from claustrophobia to community. "Only connect" is a tall order, but one that Laurence believes in.

*A Jest of God* was also significant for Laurence, because it is set in Manawaka, the mythical prairie town that she created based on her real home town of Neepawa, Manitoba. In this novel Laurence comes to terms with her ambivalence about this town, as she confronts in the character of Rachel both her need to reject and her need to retain her home. In *Heart of a Stranger*, Laurence wrote, "I had, as a child and as an adolescent, ambiguous feelings about the prairies" (4). But by the end of the novel, Rachel has freed herself from her background enough to leave Manawaka and embark for Vancouver, where she will be reunited with her sister Stacey. For a fuller discussion of setting, see the section on Manawaka.

*A Jest of God* was actually Laurence's second Manawaka novel, the first being *The Stone Angel*, arguably the greatest Canadian novel. *The Stone Angel*, published in 1964, was, as Margaret Atwood observes in her 1988 afterword to *A Jest of God*, a very hard act to follow. But *A Jest of God* was critical because it proved that Laurence's brilliant success with *The Stone Angel* was not just a flash in the pan. Atwood judges it "an almost perfect book," for, "In *A Jest of God*, Laurence does not put a foot wrong" (213–14). Certainly *A Jest of God* validates Laurence's ability both as a psychologist with profound insight into the human psyche and as an artist with unique talent for recreating the human experience.

*A Jest of God* is clearly important to the reader as well as to the author for several reasons. First, it recreates for the reader the reality of a small town in Canada, for Manawaka is a state of mind and we have all inhabited it. Second, *A Jest of God* is a *bildungsroman*, a novel about growing up, because Rachel Cameron is in a state of arrested development. She has finally reached adolescence at the age of thirty-four, when she faces her sexual initiation. In *A Jest of God* Laurence explores human psychology and examines female sexuality. As Laurence takes us behind the outward façade and into the living mind of this woman, we come to understand the reality of her being and, through her, our own. Thus Laurence not only helps us to understand ourselves, but she also teaches us how to empathize with another human being very different from ourselves — the whole purpose of fiction after all. Rachel and her sister Stacey must both master this ventriloquism of the imagination. And so must we.

*A Jest of God*, published in 1966, is also a period piece, reminding us of the traditional expectations of women. Laurence both explores and explodes the old-fashioned stereotype of the spinster schoolteacher. As Rachel reflects, "Women like me are an anachronism" (117). But Atwood reminds us that "Rachel is not some sort of aberration but merely the epitome of what nice girls were once educated to be." Rachel's faults are just "virtues gone sour: filial devotion, self-sacrifice, the concern for appearances advocated by Saint Paul, a sense of duty, the desire to avoid hurting others, and the wish to be loved" (214).

Margaret Laurence was a sexual pioneer in *A Jest of God* because she explores female sexuality and challenges the old double standard. By depicting a woman's sexual awakening and examining the forbidden issues of contraception, abortion, and single parenthood, Laurence makes feminist history. So *A Jest of God* plays a major part in the history of the development of feminism in Canada and elsewhere, as the following review of the critical reception will verify.

*A Jest of God* is also important in helping to develop the contemporary novel, for Laurence carries psychoanalysis to new depths in her exploration of the human psyche and female sexuality. Her use of interior monologue and stream of consciousness to recreate the "deep theatre" (90) of the mind delineates the differences between internal and external reality, between outer speech and inner thought. Laurence's use of polyphonic narrative through the many voices of Rachel Cameron records the complex cultural voice of Canada. Laurence also raises the Canadian novel to new artistic heights in *A Jest of God* by recreating both inner and outer reality through vivid imagery, rich allusions, and profoundly poetic language.

# Critical Reception

*A Jest of God* was an immediate triumph for Margaret Laurence, winning the Governor General's Gold Medal for Fiction in 1966 — perhaps partly in belated recognition of her brilliant first Canadian novel, *The Stone Angel*. Soon after the publication of *A Jest of God*, Paul Newman purchased the film rights and made his directing debut in his 1969 version of Laurence's novel, *Rachel, Rachel*, starring Joanne Woodward — thus emphasizing the novel's contemporary relevance.

*A Jest of God* was Laurence's second Manawaka novel, following *The Stone Angel* (1964), possibly the greatest Canadian novel to date. So the big question for *A Jest of God* was, as Atwood puts it, "if a hard act could be followed." Atwood concludes that "It could" (211). But not everyone was quite so sure. Hagar Shipley, the matriarchal protagonist of *The Stone Angel*, was so powerful a figure that the minor tones of Rachel Cameron's character and the artistic subtleties of *A Jest of God* were not immediately appreciated by reviewers.

Laurence was ahead of her time in *A Jest of God* in psychological, feminist, and artistic terms, and it has taken her critics three decades to catch up with her. Reviewers in the late sixties were simply not ready for her vivid portrayal of a middle-aged woman's sexual awakening and her confrontation with the problems of contraception, pregnancy, and abortion resulting from her first love affair — especially at a time when Canadian middle-class society officially disapproved of both extra-marital sex and single parenthood. We can trace an interesting development in the critical reception of *A Jest of God* from the earliest reviews in the late sixties, through the warmer appreciation of the seventies, to the enthusiastic response of the eighties. The critical reception of *A Jest of God* offers us a history of

Canada's intellectual, cultural, and literary development.

The Governor General's Award was rather misleading, then, for the initial reception of the novel was critical indeed. In a 1967 review entitled "Lack of Distance," Robert Harlow offers a chauvinist response: "I find myself suddenly applauding with only one hand" (189), because he judges "this book is a failure" (190).

> Rachel is monolithic. Her character is carpeted wail-to-wail with her failures. Unable to be loveable, she is not loved; physically unattractive, socially inept, sexually fearful, one could imagine a psychiatrist giving up and uttering that famous line: "Let's face it, you *are* inferior."
>
> What is lacking — and even the difficult first person present tense technique, if properly used, could handle this fault — is objectivity, distance, irony. One simply gets tired of listening to Rachel taking pot-shots at herself. The reader, instead of identifying, finds himself (herself, too, I should think) silently shouting at her to get some eye-liner, save for a mink, strong-arm a man, kill her mother and stop bitching. (190)

In *Margaret Laurence* (1967), the first book devoted to Laurence's writing, Laurence critic and admirer Clara Thomas finds herself regretfully agreeing with Harlow's judgement and "applaud[ing] with one hand only" (53). Thomas compares Rachel Cameron with Hagar Shipley as "no tragic heroine, but an ordinary foolish mortal" (49). She judges that "artistically, as a novel, [*A Jest of God*] slides out of balance. Because everything comes through Rachel's consciousness and because her mind is so completely, believably, neurotically obsessed, she cannot really see the world around her or the people in it" (51).

That, of course, is the point: Laurence shows us the schizophrenic character waking up to reality, as the narrative technique recreates this psychological development dramatically. The negative criticism of *A Jest of God* in the late sixties focuses on the innovative narrative method which Laurence defends thus: "*A Jest of God*, as some critics have pointed out disapprovingly, is a very inturned novel. I recognize the limitations of a novel told in the first person and the present tense, from one viewpoint only, but it couldn't have been done any other way, for Rachel herself is a very inturned person" ("Ten" 21).

The reaction to this early negative response set in quickly. The year after Harlow's slam, H.J. Rosengarten responded in a 1968 review entitled "Inescapable Bonds." He accused Harlow of a reading that was not only unsympathetic but simplistic because it missed the point of the novel, namely Rachel's inner conflict and the ensuing irony:

> To suggest that there is a lack of objectivity is to ignore the corrective distance presented within the character's own view of herself, the moral perspective that is provided by Rachel's dual consciousness. . . . The drama of Rachel's struggle and failure is played out entirely within her consciousness, but the narrowness of the point of view does not limit the novel's meaning. The theme of individual aspiration conquered by social convention and personal guilt is all the more forcibly conveyed by this intense concentration on a single sensibility. (192–93)

Rosengarten's sensitive reading of *A Jest of God* pointed the way for the critics of the early seventies, who appreciate both the psychological and the artistic brilliance of Laurence's novel. Canadian author George Bowering began the tradition of perceptive discussions of this imaginative novel by creative writers with his insightful 1971 essay, "That Fool of a Fear: Notes on *A Jest of God*." Bowering specifically rejects the early negative reviews of Laurence's novel: "In *A Jest of God*, seen as formally failed by some nineteenth-century reviewers, Margaret Laurence assays a responsive vocal style, the voice in the ear pursuing Rachel's mind even into the deep places where the most superior fiction . . . comes from" (210). He particularly admires Laurence's narrative method:

> So I praise the process, beginning with place and voice, leading to that third thing hard to name, something like the risk or gift of getting naked, so that your nakedness may touch something that is not yours. The form of the novel, first person and present tense, works as Rachel's opening-out does, to get naked. Margaret Laurence shows uncommon courage making this book, to confront social and deep personal stupidities and fears in the womb of her narrator. (211)

He concludes, "God's jests are not just vocal — the word is made flesh, i.e., the eternal present. It is in understanding this that Margaret

Laurence chose wisely to write in the present tense, to present the fool made wise by folly. God's grace shines on fools. Poetry is hospitable to the fool's tongue, and *vice versa*. Rachel's acceptance speech is poetry" (225–26).

Focusing on form rather than content, Bowering praises Laurence's artistry in *A Jest of God*, recognizing Canadian fiction's artistic coming of age and claiming that "Margaret Laurence is the rare Canadian writer who shows a care for the novel as good writing, language shaped to find literature" (210).

> One of the reasons for my attention to *A Jest of God* is the seriousness of the work as literature. Margaret Laurence is an unusual bird among Canadian novelists, in that she works on the premise that form (not "structure") matters pre-eminently in the endeavour to simulate reality. What happens happens *in* the writing, not in front of it. One sees through the eye, not with it. Laurence is not talking *about* life; she is trying to re-enact the responses to it. I differ from most commentators in praising the success of the present tense and the interior, confused, first person narrative. The subject of the book is Rachel's mind, and the realism consists in our separation from it by virtue of its unsureness and confusions. That separation brings us so close, because we are in the position of wanting to talk to Rachel. (223–24)

In the early seventies, critics recognized *A Jest of God* as an essentially humanist text, with Rachel Cameron representing the suffering human condition, rather than viewing the novel, as critics have done in the late eighties, as an ultimately feminist text, with Rachel as female pioneer. In 1971, C.M. McLay acknowledges, "While Rachel's predicament is essentially feminine, it is also human" (188). Her title, "Every Man Is an Island" — paraphrasing John Donne's maxim, "No man is an island" — emphasizes the human condition of isolation that McLay sees as the major theme, rather than the female sex of the protagonist:

> Margaret Laurence in *A Jest of God* suggests a complementary truth, that every man is an island, a theme more typical of the twentieth century. . . . It is her recognition of this overwhelming truth that frees Rachel from her past failures, with her father,

with her mother, even with Nick, and enables her to face her future with fortitude. And it is Laurence's ability to capture this truth, to recreate in fiction the sense of isolation, where human beings reach out to each other and reach out futilely, which makes *A Jest of God* and the earlier *The Stone Angel* notable achievements in Canadian and in world literature. (177–78)

In his introduction to the New Canadian Library edition of *A Jest of God* in 1974, G.D. Killam follows McLay's lead by emphasizing Rachel's humanity: "Freedom, survival, communication these are the problems the book deals with and they are common to mankind" (n. pag.). In her 1976 book, *The Manawaka World of Margaret Laurence*, Clara Thomas also emphasizes Rachel Cameron's common humanity: Rachel represents "the cruelly caricatured 'old maid' humanized and dignified, the author's insistent voice saying behind Rachel's own, 'this is a person, certainly flimsy and perhaps gutless, no heroics, no Promethean pride here, but a living human being, capable of growth and demanding respect. Attention must be paid' " (79). Rachel Cameron has become the *anti-heroine*: "Rachel's real salvation and significance is that she is not a tragic figure, not the character in a drama that she sometimes makes of herself, but just an ordinary human being" (85).

The next book devoted to Laurence's writing, the Twayne *Margaret Laurence* by Patricia Morley in 1981, points the way to the new direction of the eighties with its emphasis on the polyphonic quality of the novel and the feminist focus of its protagonist. Morley responds to Harlow as a touchstone, observing that "Harlow misses the multiple voices of Rachel, who thinks and voices a very complex self" (90). Morley also points to the feminist focus of the novel:

Rachel's story, and all the Manawaka works, dramatize the plight of women in a male-oriented, chauvinistic society where both sexes are often unconscious of bias and social conditioning. Hagar's experience could be transposed into a male key with relatively minor alterations, but Rachel's is inescapably female. Her basic insecurity and passivity, her financial anxiety, her sexual vulnerability in the event of pregnancy, and her responsibility for her mother (a situation called by some feminists "the compassion trap") are all traditional female dilemmas. (91–92)

Recent criticism of *A Jest of God* in the late eighties has focused on the novel as a feminist text. Margaret Atwood, in her 1988 afterword to the new edition of the novel, finds Laurence's 1966 text relevant to contemporary women:

> Re-reading *A Jest of God* yet again, I was cheered by how little it has dated. Some of the social customs and sexual constraints may have vanished, but the kinds of expectations placed on women, although in different costume, are still around — perfect physical beauty, total self-confidence, angelic and selfless nurturing of one variety or another. What Rachel can offer us now as readers is something we still need to know: how to acknowledge our own human and necessary limitations, our own foolishness. How to say both No, and Yes. (215)

Atwood sees Rachel's experience as a constructive lesson for contemporary women.

Canadian novelist Aritha Van Herk, in "The Eulalias of Spinsters and Undertakers" in *Crossing the River: Essays in Honour of Margaret Laurence* offers an even more explicitly feminist reading. Focusing on the spinster schoolteacher stereotype employed by early critics of the novel, Van Herk judges that "the novel as cry has been largely mis-heard, de-cried by a childish encoding of a word from one of those brutal nursery rhymes." She cites Harlow as "the archetypal male reader" with a "phallocentric ear" who cannot hear Rachel's female voice in his "churlish" review (134–35). Van Herk offers a feminist reading which unites Rachel's religious glossalalia with her orgasmic eulalia — "Eulalia: a woman's cry at the moment of orgasm" (133) — "*A Jest of God* gives novelistic tongue to a language that silences the body and to a language that speaks the body," for "*A Jest of God* undertakes to unearth Rachel's eulalia, long-buried: her glossalalia that cries out to God/father/lover/mortician for hearing" (134). Van Herk concludes:

> . . . Rachel's tongue has been unloosed, and she can call the language of the future. . . . She has freed her speech, opened her mouth, cried out in that vocabulary that can never be glossed, that voice ululating its own longing. Rachel's cry echoes past its origin: her speaking offers the tongues of men and angels to all

the heroines who have followed her eulalic story. Her bones have been opened, broken; they can now rejoice. (144)

Far from apologizing for Rachel's humanity, critics now hail her as a heroine.

At the 1988 Margaret Laurence Memorial Conference at the University of Brandon, Manitoba, three papers were devoted to *A Jest of God*, more than to any other single work by Laurence, and all focused on Rachel's feminine heroism and Laurence's polyphonic narrative. We can deduce that this richly imaginative and artistic novel will continue to attract creative criticism.

# Reading of the Text

## MANAWAKA: "A TOWN OF THE MIND"

Manitoba means "God's Plenty," but Manawaka, the place where *A Jest of God* is set, is a name Margaret Laurence invented for her model town, which is based on her home town of Neepawa, a small prairie town near Winnipeg in Manitoba. Manawaka, where Rachel Cameron lives, may be the novel's true antagonist, the enemy from whom Rachel must wrest her freedom, for Manawaka is what Laurence called "a town of the mind, my own private world" (*Heart* 3).

Manawaka forms the setting for most of Laurence's Canadian novels — the so-called "Manawaka Series." All of Laurence's Canadian heroines are trapped by Manawaka or escape from its manacles: Hagar Shipley in *The Stone Angel* (1964) leaves Manawaka and then returns to it; Rachel Cameron in *A Jest of God* (1966) is trapped in Manawaka until the end of the novel; in *The Fire-Dwellers* (1969), Rachel's sister Stacey has escaped Manawaka early to live in Vancouver with her salesman husband Clifford MacAindra and their four children; Laurence's youngest heroine, Vanessa MacLeod, grows up to leave Manawaka in the short-story collection *A Bird in the House* (1970); in *The Diviners* (1974), Laurence's last heroine, Morag Gunn, escapes from Manawaka, as Laurence herself did, to attend college in Winnipeg, but finally realizes, like her creator, that she carries a map of her home town inside her skull. As Laurence wrote, "these are things I will carry inside my skull for as long as I live, with the vividness of recall that only our first home can have for us" (*Heart* 4).

But Manawaka transcends Neepawa: not just *any* prairie town, it is *every* small town. Laurence explains, "Manawaka is not so much any one prairie town as an amalgam of many prairie towns" (*Heart*

3). So Manawaka is a microcosm of society, encapsulating all the conventions, repressions, and hypocrisies, as well as the fortitude, dignity, and generosity that Laurence views as typically Canadian.

Not only a microcosm, Manawaka is also a vividly real, specific place. As Laurence says, "Writing, for me, has to be set firmly in some soil, some place, some outer and inner territory which might be described in anthropological terms as 'cultural background'" (*Heart* 6). Laurence paints the town and terrain of Manawaka in vivid local colours of river and valley, trees and flowers, as well as streets and houses. Moreover, all of the features of the town and terrain represent Laurence's themes, forming a kind of moralized landscape.

Manawaka is divided by the proverbial railway tracks. But the tracks are not simply an economic boundary, dividing the town into rich and poor; they are also a moral boundary, dividing the town by class, culture, and ethnic background. Rachel explains, "Half the town is Scots descent and the other half is Ukrainian. Oil, as they say, and water. Both came for the same reasons, because they had nothing where they were before. That was a long way away and a long time ago. The Ukrainians knew how to be the better grain farmers, but the Scots knew how to be almightier than anyone but God" (65). Rachel must learn to bridge that ethnic gap or cultural chasm if she is to develop as a character.

The Camerons live on "the right side of the tracks": Rachel reflects, "This is known as a good part of town. Not like the other side of the tracks, where the shacks are and where the weeds are let grow knee-high and not dutifully mown, and where a few bootleggers drive new Chevrolets on the strength of home-made red biddy" (11). Rachel realizes, "Half my children live at that end of town. I never go there, and know it only from hearsay, distorted local legend, or the occasional glimpse from a child's words" (11). But living on the right side of the tracks turns out to be a grave disadvantage for Rachel.

When Rachel embarks on a summer romance with Nick Kazlik, son of Nestor the Jester, the Manawaka milkman, just home from Winnipeg for the summer to visit his parents, she realizes that the Slavic farmers may have been economically disadvantaged, but the proper little Scots-Presbyterian girl was deprived of more important things — of fun and freedom. She tells Nick that she envied Ukrainians for being "more resistant" and "more free." "Laying girls and doing gay Slavic dances?" (87), mocks Nick. She elaborates: "Not so boxed-in, maybe. More outspoken. More able to speak out. More allowed to — both by your family and by yourself" (88). Rachel must learn to emulate the people on the other side of the tracks if she is to escape from her personal prison of repression.

Manawaka is a state of mind, and it has become a prison for Rachel, a jail where she is enduring a life sentence. She feels trapped by repressions, hemmed in by hypocrisies, and "bounded by trivialities" (82). For example, when Rachel initiates her love affair with Nick Kazlik, who asks her to "fix" herself (93), Rachel cannot think where to go for contraceptive advice, because she fears the "prairie drums" (81) that will carry the news directly to the town gossip. Angela Siddley, the principal's wife, is "the reverse of those three wise monkeys," because "Angela hears all, sees all, and tells the whole works" (82).

In Manawaka, even God must stay on the right side of the tracks. Laurence uses churches to explore the spiritual values of Canada, as Rachel tours the religious establishments of the town. There are two main churches: the Scots-Presbyterian Church that the Camerons patronize, and the Tabernacle of the Risen and Reborn, where Rachel would prefer not to be caught dead. The two churches encapsulate the values embraced on opposite sides of the tracks. In contrast to the Presbyterian Church's tasteful stained-glass window depicting "a pretty and clean-cut Jesus expiring gently and with absolutely no inconvenience, no gore, no pain, just this nice and slightly effeminate insurance salesman" (41), the Tabernacle depicts a human, suffering Jesus, "bearded and bleeding, his heart exposed and bristling with thorns like a scarlet pincushion" (30).

Rachel attends the Presbyterian Church each Sunday morning, although she claims not to believe, just for the sake of appearances and to please her mother who thinks it would not "look very good" if Rachel, as a school teacher, did not attend church (39). May Cameron enjoys church primarily as a social club: "She loves coming to church because she sees everyone, and in spring the new hats are like a forest of tulips. But as for faith — I suppose she takes it for granted that she believes. Yet if the Reverend MacElfrish should suddenly lose his mind and speak of God with anguish or joy, or out of some need should pray with fierce humility as though God had to be there, Mother would be shocked to the core. Luckily, it will never happen" (41). Since "anyone speaking in a clarion voice about their

beliefs ... seems indecent" (26), Reverend MacElfrish delivers a safe
sermon on Gratitude in a smooth, mellifluous voice: "He says we are
fortunate to be living here, in plenty, and we ought not to take our
blessings for granted. Who is likely to quibble with that?" (41).

The Tabernacle of the Risen and Reborn, in contrast, has all of the
colour and zest that Rachel envied in the Ukrainians on the other
side of the tracks. Housed in a fanciful edifice, "encrusted with
glassed-in porches, pillars with no purpose, wrought-iron balconies
... a small turret or two for good measure, and the blue and red glass
circle of a rose-window at the very top" (29), the Tabernacle boasts
a bright crimson sign out front, like a nightclub, advertising "*Tabernacle of the Risen and Reborn*" (29). Whereas the Presbyterian
Church proclaims good taste in everything from its sober carillon
tinkling "The Church's One Foundation" to its understated, expen-
sive furnishings (40–41), the Tabernacle boasts a florid pulpit "bulky
and new, pale wood blossoming in bunches of grapes and small sharp
birds with beaks uplifted ... draped with white velvet, like a scarf,
tasselled with limp silver threads," and holding a Bible, "not jacketed
severely in black but covered with some faintly glittering cloth or
substance impersonating gold," as if it might "give off sparks" (30).
Rachel concludes, "[t]he Tabernacle has too much gaudiness and
zeal, and [the Church] has too little" (41). So Rachel must find her
own truth amid this conflict of spiritual values.

The other important edifice in the authority structure of the town
and in Rachel's own life is the school where Rachel teaches grade two.
The novel opens in the schoolroom, with Rachel looking out through
the window to the playground, where she sees her pupils singing the
same skipping songs she sang in the same playground when she
herself was seven years old, exactly twenty-seven years ago. But now
Rachel's role is reversed, and she is "the thin giant She" with "the
power" (1). Rachel may have the power, but she feels imprisoned in
this school where she has been trapped for fourteen years in a
perpetual childhood. She thinks, "I would like to leave this school"
(25), but she does not have the courage to break out of the childish
cocoon in which she has been enclosed.

Even Rachel's bedroom is unchanged since her childhood: "This
bedroom is the same I've always had. I should change the furniture.
How girlish it is, how old-fashioned. The white spindly-legged
dressing-table, the round mirror with white rose-carved frame, the

white-painted metal bed with its white-painted metal bow decorating the head like a starched forgotten hair-ribbon" (16). The virginal decor of the room is appropriate, for Rachel is an arrested adolescent.

The most important building, of course, is the Cameron Funeral Home, so ironically named, where Rachel lives with her aging mother "above the store." "Death's unmentionable" (122) in polite society, Rachel insists, and so death is not allowed across the tracks that divide upper-class Scots Manawaka from the lower-class ethnic town: "No one in Manawaka ever dies, at least not on this side of the tracks. We are a gathering of immortals. We pass on, through Calla's divine gates of topaz and azure, perhaps, but we do not die. Death is rude, unmannerly, not to be spoke to in the street" (13). Perhaps that is why the dead are "painted and prettified" (2) by morticians like Niall Cameron in an attempt to deny "the skull beneath the skin" (122). But it is difficult for Rachel, "the undertaker's daughter" (67), to deny the fact of death, living as she does, above the town funeral parlour.

Rachel's home is a graphic symbol of life and death, for the mortuary is on the ground floor and the Camerons' living quarters are in the upstairs flat — a metaphor for the different planes of existence. Rachel's father goes underground literally, preferring the company of the "unspeaking ones" (13) downstairs to his even colder wife upstairs. May Cameron attempts to deny the fact of death, flitting about like a waspish angel with a feather duster. She even covers the furniture where her husband sits with crocheted doilies so that death will not rub off on her home, for fear the family might catch the germ of death from him.

Walking home one night along Japonica Street and up the primrose path where the mortuary sign beckons, Rachel realizes, "I see all at once how laughable it is, to live here, how funny lots of people must think it, how amusing, how hilarious" (56). She thinks, "I must get out of here" (56), and even declares to Nick, "I hate living here" (68). No matter how fiercely she fears foolishness, however, Rachel lacks life to leave this house of death.

The only distinctive feature of Rachel's rust brick home is the sign out front advertising death. The permutations of the sign reflect polite society's gradual denial of death. In Rachel's father's day, the sign spelled "Cameron's Funeral Parlour" in sombre black letters on pale-grey background. But later, Niall Cameron, laughing sardonically, changed the sign to read "Cameron Funeral Home" in elegant gilt letters on ebony background — no doubt to underline the irony of his dying marriage. Niall Cameron's successor, Hector Jonas, replaces the still sombre sign with a flowery one flashing "Japonica Funeral Chapel" in blue neon lights that flicker on and off automatically, "like the delphinium blinking of eyes" (68). Rachel reflects, "All that remains is for someone to delete the word *funeral*. A nasty word, smacking of mortality" (13). And that is precisely what happens. At the end of the novel, Hector proudly presents his new neon sign cheerfully flashing "Japonica Chapel" in crimson lights, like a night club, purged forever of the sinister word "funeral" (200). Rachel comments, tactfully but truthfully, "It's a change, Hector. It's — evolution" (201).

Nature always provides a refuge for Laurence's characters, and Rachel loves the sheltering spruce trees in front of the mortuary on Japonica Street, where she can hide from prying eyes: "Around our place the spruce trees still stand, as I remember them for ever. No other trees are so darkly sheltering, shutting out prying eyes or the sun in summer, the spearheads of them taller than houses, the low branches heavy, reaching down to the ground like the greenblack feathered strong-boned wings of giant and extinct birds" (13). Rachel even locates her fantasy encounter with "[t]he shadow prince" under the sheltering green fronds of evergreen trees (18–19) — the only place where she feels safe.

The landscape surrounding Manawaka is almost as important as the town itself in *A Jest of God*, for Laurence employs features of the terrain as a moralized landscape to symbolize her themes. Laurence writes that Manawaka "has elements of Neepawa, especially in some of the descriptions of places, such as the cemetery on the hill or the Wachakwa valley" (*Heart* 3). The Wachakwa River Valley is the source of natural vitality, in contrast to the deadly repressions of the town. When Nick and Steve Kazlik want to find "neutral territory" (86), they repair to the river. And when James Doherty plays hookey from school, he escapes to the valley. When Rachel and Nick make love, they seek the banks of the Wachakwa where they are protected from prying eyes and gossiping tongues by "bluffs of poplar with their always-whispering leaves that are touched into sound by even the slightest wind, and choke-cherry bushes with the clusters of berries still hard and green, and matted screens of wild rose bushes with nearly all their petals fallen, only the yellow dying centre remaining" (83). Rachel and Nick can glimpse the cemetery from the valley where they make love, however, suggesting the essential connection between life and death.


## SPINSTERS AND SPECTRES

Margaret Laurence's greatest genius is for creating characters. Her female protagonists are particularly realistic because they represent facets of their creator's character, although Laurence respects the autonomy of her heroines:

> . . . for a writer of fiction, part of the heart remains that of a stranger, for what we are trying to do is to understand those others who are our fictional characters, somehow to gain entrance to their minds and feelings, to respect them for themselves as human individuals, and to portray them as truly as we can. The whole process of fiction is a mysterious one, and a writer, however experienced, remains in some ways a perpetual amateur, or perhaps a perpetual traveller, an explorer of those inner territories, those strange lands of the heart and spirit. (*Heart* vii–viii)

In *A Jest of God*, Laurence enters the mind of her heroine to demonstrate that the heart of a stranger may be the spirit of a friend.


### Rachel Cameron

Rachel Cameron, the central character of *A Jest of God*, is a thirty-four-year-old unmarried schoolteacher who still lives with her mother above the funeral parlour where her father was the proprietor. On the death of her father, the alcoholic undertaker Niall Cameron, fourteen years previously, Rachel returned home to Manawaka from university in Winnipeg to keep house for her hypochondriac mother, May, and she has remained there ever since. Rachel's real enemy, the true antagonist of the novel, is the town, for Manawaka imprisons Rachel with manacles of repression that stifle her freedom.

Rachel is a paranoid protagonist, for she is crippled by imaginary fears: "I honestly do not know why I feel the daft sting of imagined embarrassments. The ones that occur are more than plenty, God knows" (61). A chronic worrier, she is always "anticipating that worst which never happens, at least not in the way one imagines" (31). She also torments herself with remembered humiliations: "All such words cling to the mind like burrs to hair, and I can never seem to brush them away, as I know I should do" (138).

Rachel is truly paranoid, for she is afraid of everything, even insanity. A stereotypical spinster schoolteacher, she fears the neurosis that she believes threatens single women. She stops herself when she finds her mind wandering obsessively in morbid imaginings: "There. I am doing it again. This must stop. It isn't good for me. Whenever I find myself thinking in a brooding way, I must simply turn it off and think of something else. God forbid that I should turn into an eccentric" (2). Hanging on to sanity by her fingernails, she is obsessed with fear of madness: "Am I doing it again, this waking nightmare? How weird am I already? Trying to stave off something that has already grown inside me and spread its roots through my blood?" (17). *A Jest of God* records Rachel's struggle to save her sanity and survive.

Symptomatic of Rachel's neurosis is her distorted perception of reality. She realizes that "Something must be the matter with my way of viewing things" because "The darkening sky is hugely blue, gashed with rose, blood, flame pouring from the volcano or wound or flower of the lowering sun. The wavering green, the sea of grass, piercingly bright. Black tree trunks, contorted, arching over the river" (85). Both her inner and outer reality are paranoid and apocalyptic: "When I close my eyes, I see scratches of gold against the black, and they form into jagged lines, teeth, a knife's edge, the sharp hard hackles of dinosaurs" (59).

Consciousness for Rachel is *"Hell on wheels,"* and she is bound to the clock's nocturnal circling as to a cosmic Catherine wheel: "The night feels like a gigantic ferris wheel turning in blackness, very slowly, turning once for each hour, interminably slow. And I am glued to it, or wired, like paper, like a photograph, insubstantial, unable to anchor myself, unable to stop this slow nocturnal circling" (18). Consciousness is such a waking nightmare for Rachel that she craves the oblivion of death or the little death of sleep: *"Each day dies with sleep.* I wish it did. My headache has gone, but I'm restless. The slow whirling begins again, the night's wheel that turns and turns, pointlessly" (58).

Rachel worries, "Am I unbalanced? Or only laughable? That's worse, much worse" (19). More than madness, Rachel fears being a fool: "I'm not a fool" (46), she insists. She loathes seeing other people make fools of themselves: "I can't bear watching people make fools of themselves. I don't know why, but it threatens me. It swamps me, and I can't look, the way as children we used to cover our eyes with our hands at the dreaded parts in horror movies" (27). Her most painful experiences involve witnessing octogenarian Tom Gillanders sing a solo or remembering the Dukes's mongoloid son using swear words in church (42): "How can they make fools of themselves like that, so publicly?" (10). She loathes living above the mortuary because "I see all at once how laughable it is, to live here, how funny lots of people must think it, how amusing, how hilarious" (56).

The source of Rachel's fear of foolishness is the small-town emphasis on appearances — how things will *look* — at its strongest on Sundays. When Rachel declined to attend church because she did not believe, her mother demurred, "I don't think it would be very nice, not to go. I don't think it would look very good" (39). Manawaka's Scots-Presbyterian church portrays God as "Big Brother Watching You." So Rachel is obsessed with eyes watching her: running "the gauntlet of eyes," she imagines "the eyes all around have swollen to giants' eyes" (48) and that everyone is looking at her — even the "golden cats with seeing eyes" (59) of her fantasies and the corpses with their "glass eyes, cat's eye marbles, round glass beads, blue and milky, unwinking" (19) of her nightmares.

Rachel is paranoid because she is alienated from other people, especially her former pupils: "They seem like a different race, a separate species, all those generations of children," Rachel reflects. The skipping song the children sing — *"Spanish dancers, turn around, / Spanish dancers, get out of this town"* (1) — underlines Rachel's sense of exclusion. Although Rachel feels her pupils are her children, they disappear at the end of each year to be metamorphosed into adolescent aliens. Two teenage girls with lacquered beehive hairdos look to Rachel like "twins from outer space" or "Venusians" (12) invading her planet.

Observing some teenage girls' eyes, masked with makeup "blue-green like the sea," Rachel wonders, "What do those plain eyes in their jewelled setting see?" (55). Since her students have already learned "to mock automatically" (5), she fears "the confident dismissal of their eyes" (55): "Does thirty-four seem antediluvian to them? Why did they laugh? There isn't anything to be frightened of, in that laughter. Why should they have meant anything snide by it?" (12). Intruding on Rachel's reverie, the girls giggle nervously at her abstraction, but their innocent greeting appears to the paranoid protagonist as ridicule. When one threatening creature gives Rachel an innocent greeting — "Hello, Miss Cameron" — Rachel meditates: "Whoever she once was — that's long gone. Some child I was drawn to, perhaps and may have shown it, and she remembers and can't forgive it, for she detests now and would like to kill for ever the little girl who believed it was really something if the teacher was pleased with the work she'd done" (55–56). Such paranoia is truly insane. Perhaps Rachel is threatened by teenagers because she herself has failed to mature beyond adolescence.

Rachel hardly inhabits the real world, so threatening does it appear. She is so alienated from reality that she prefers to live in her own imagination, in the "deep theatre" (90) of the mind, where "I dramatize myself" (4). But this inner theatre is dangerous too, for the paranoid Rachel imagines "an unseen audience ready to hoot and caw with a shocking derision" (95). Not even the star of her own drama, the heroine of her own life, Rachel is an uneasy extra, fearing ridicule. Nor is she in control of her private theatre, for the willed masturbation fantasy of the "shadow prince" (18) gives way to the involuntary nightmare of the kingdom of death, where corpses powdered like clowns stare at her with glass eyes, their rouged lips twitching to mock her terror (19).

Rachel is schizophrenic, a dual personality. The 1969 film version of *A Jest of God* was appropriately titled *Rachel, Rachel,* because there are two Rachels, and they live in two different worlds, seen through opposite ends of a telescope. Rachel reflects, "I have no middle view. Either I fix on a detail and see it as though it were magnified — a leaf with all its veins perceived, the fine hairs on the back of a man's hands — or else the world recedes and becomes blurred, artificial, indefinite, an abstract painting of a world" (85). She worries, "If you think you contain two realities, perhaps you contain none" (133).

Nick Kazlik is not the only character with a phantom twin, for Rachel is a "divided self," in the terms of R.D. Laing. She acknowledges, "I dramatize myself. I always did. No one would ever know it from the outside, where I'm too quiet" (4). Doubly divided, Rachel addresses herself as a separate person, saying, "We have discussed this a long time ago, you and I, Rachel" (71). Proof of her doubleness is the fact that she talks to herself in the mirror.

Mirrors reflect her double image, frightening her with her own duality: "I can't succeed in avoiding my eyes in the mirror. The narrow angular face stares at me, the grey eyes too wide for it" (16). Rachel panics when she addresses her reflection in the mirror: "In the long wall mirror I saw myself running, the white of my dress, the featureless face, the tallness, a thin stiff white feather like a goose's feather, caught up and hurtled along by some wind no one else could feel" (153). Rachel is frightened by the ghostly implications when she sees herself reflected in a store window, wearing her white hooded raincoat — "a thin streak of a person, like the stroke of a white chalk on a blackboard," "like the negative of a photograph" (29) — her *doppelgänger* or double. Scarcely a material girl, Rachel is not sure if she is even alive.

The implications are appropriate, for Rachel is a zombie, one of the walking dead. Repressed out of reality by Manawaka's mores, Rachel is not really living, but merely existing. No wonder that one suitor, a salesman in embalming fluid, admired her for her "good bones" — "as though he were one of the ancient Egyptians who interred the pharaohs and knew too intimately the secrets of the core and marrow" (17) — because Rachel has been literally entombed all her life in the Cameron Funeral Home, a name ironic in its accuracy.

Driven underground to a living death or hell on earth by her repressive environment, Rachel's stifled psyche surfaces in fantasies and nightmares. The first chapter concludes with a vivid fantasy of a "shadow prince," revealing Rachel's frustrated sexuality. Her suppressed fear of death also materializes in nightmares of her father ruling as king of the dead in the mortuary that lurks downstairs, just beneath the surface of her conscious mind (18–19).

Rachel's real voice is also stifled in interior monologues. Her only real outcries are silent screams, rendered in emphatic italics: *"My God. How can I stand — "* (17). When she does speak, it is in artificial or borrowed voices. Not until the turning-point of the novel will

Rachel's inner and outer voices unite, when she enters the real world, as we will see in the chapter, "Themes: 'Surviving with Dignity.'" Meanwhile, the only person she can talk to is a God she claims not to believe in.

Repressed maternally, sexually, and spiritually, Rachel is like a volcano ready to explode. And she does explode both verbally and physically in school and in church. In school, she strikes her favourite pupil, James Doherty, with a ruler, making his nose bleed. Rachel's voice, long stifled in the crypt on Japonica Street, finally surfaces in cryptic cries in the Tabernacle of the Risen and Reborn (29), where the *"gift of tongues"* has been given to the congregation. Rachel fears that Calla will "suddenly rise and keen like the Grecian women wild on the hills" (31), but it is Rachel who finds her tongue: "Not Calla's voice. Mine. Oh my God. Mine. The voice of Rachel" (36).

The voice of Rachel is "mourning for her children" (181), like her Biblical namesake. A childless spinster, Rachel calls her pupils "my children" (2), even though she knows she must not. But Rachel is not ready to be a mother because she is still a child, as Calla's continual epithet "Child" reminds us. Rachel's bedroom is still the frilly room of her girlhood (16). She is in a state of arrested development, trapped in adolescence. Imprisoned in an ageless no-man's-land, Rachel reflects, "What a strangely pendulum life I have, fluctuating in age between extremes, hardly knowing myself whether I am too young or too old" (57). Sexually inexperienced, Rachel realizes, "Women like me are an anachronism" (117). She cannot grow up into adult independence because she is still dominated by her hypochondriac mother and dead father.

### May Cameron

May Cameron represses Rachel through the old-fashioned values that she has bequeathed her daughter, especially her emphasis on appearances — on how things will *look* and what people will *say*: "'Didn't you think it might look — well, just a little peculiar?' Not — was it peculiar? Only — did it look so?" (167). She also disapproves of sex, especially outside of marriage, judging Cassie Stewart's twins a "heartbreak for her mother" (58). She drilled into Rachel the old cliché that virginity was *"A woman's most precious possession"* (89–90) so firmly that Rachel's virginity has become a millstone around her neck. "I thank my lucky stars I never had a moment's worry with either of my daughters" (58), she observes, prompting Rachel to reflect resentfully, "Had. Past tense" (58).

Her bad heart is the main source of the power Mrs. Cameron wields over her daughter Rachel. As Margaret Atwood says, she "plays guilt like a violin" (214). And the tune she plays is hearts and flowers, obliging Rachel to be "careful of her, as though to preserve her throughout eternity, a dried flower under glass" (195). Rachel is even afraid to go out, lest her mother have a heart attack in her absence and die, "and then I would have been forever in the wrong" (73). So the only excursions Rachel is allowed are guilt trips.

May Cameron is symbolized by the colour mauve, appropriate for aging femininity. Even her veins are violet, suggesting that she is not red-blooded or blue-blooded, but somewhere in between. She "lifts one violet-veined wrist and lets it fall, driftingly slow. . . . [t]he lady of the camellias, dying on silver screen, *circa* 1930" (194), Rachel reflects. But violet is also the vivid colour her mouth becomes when she has a heart attack (39) — "that worrying purple that tinges her mouth like potassium permanganate" (62) — symbolizing her mortality.

Mrs. Cameron embodies the old-fashioned stereotype of femininity: "Her hair is done every week, saucily stiff grey sausage curls, and the frames of her glasses are delphinium blue and elfin. Where does this cuteness come from?" (14), wonders Rachel. Named for spring, May Cameron, "in her new flowered-silk coat walks along like a butterfly released from winter," making Rachel feel in contrast "like some lean greyhound being led out for a walk" (40). Her mother's "archaic simper voice" (90) is falsely feminine, "meadowlarking" (39) about the mortuary in a parody of springtime. Even in her dreams, Rachel hears her mother "singing in a falsetto voice, the stylish tremolo, the ladies' choir voice. *Bless this house dear Lord we pray, keep it safe by night and day*" (19).

Rachel remarks, "She is amazing for her age" (40) — although Rachel does not even know how old her mother is, since May Cameron, no longer a spring chicken, is vain and secretive about her age. "No one could say mortality had very noticeably laid claws on her, not yet" (62), Rachel reflects, even though her mother is seventy at least and has long since joined the blue-rinse brigade. Long past the buttons and bows stage of stereotypical feminine cuteness, she has graduated to lavender and old lace. She surrounds herself with them, coaxing her sparse locks into a "grey lace" (73) around her face when she goes to bed wearing alluring mauve nylon nightgowns, although her husband is long dead.

Even doing her housework, she seems to be "dusting in small feathery strokes as though the duster were a chiffon handkerchief and she were waving it from some castle window" (75), like the Lady of Shalott, to "make the house look as though no frail and mortal creature ever set foot in it" (15). She even covers the furniture with crocheted lace doilies so that no one, especially her husband, can touch her furniture — or, by extension, herself.

The paraphernalia of her house reveals her kitschy character, as she straightens the pictures, "one small white mauve-veined hand on the autumn-coloured print of The Strawberry Girl," and then adjusts "a simpering puce-mouthed Madonna" (67) resembling herself. When Rachel ransacks her mother's dresser, "like a she-Goth out for loot," searching for her mother's archaic contraceptive contraption, she unearths pathetically feminine relics:

Small blue glass bottles, once *Evening in Paris* but long since dried; a stack of heavy clotted-lace doilies she crocheted for the arms of chairs and never used, having a million others; new nylon nightgowns, pink pastel, still folded in the tissue paper, given to her by my sister each Christmas, but believed too delicate to wear — morbidly, she saves them for hospital and the last illness, so she'll die demurely; a sachet of rose petals encased in stiff mauve voile and tied with a royal purple ribbon, the petals now ruined to the appearance of bran flakes; a chocolate box filled with sepia photographs of herself, a ringleted child with enormous long-lashed eyes and prettily pursed mouth. . . . (98)

This dresser drawer looks like a coffin containing May's blighted spring.

The same attitudes that repressed Rachel also killed May's marriage and her husband, turning Niall Cameron into a zombie. "One thing about your father, he was never one to make many demands on me," May remarks, making Rachel reflect, "how terrible for him" (90). She stifled any form of communication between them: Rachel recalls, "She and Dad had given up conversing long ago, by the time I was born" (16). "Her weapons are invisible" (40), Rachel realizes, but with these invisible weapons she drained all the blood out of her husband, until he became such a zombie that he was more at home with the stiffs downstairs. Holding a private party with his silent company in the mortuary, he pours in alcohol to replace the blood in his veins — like a mortician's embalming fluid.

It is not until she hears her mother murmur sleepily, *Niall always thinks I am so stupid"* (186), that Rachel realizes that there may have been two sides to that old story. Eventually she even comes to realize that it takes two to play her mother's power games. When Rachel finally gains enough confidence to view her mother with compassion, she recognizes that her mother is not powerful but pathetic. She realizes that "She cares about me" (94), and that is why she naturally worries about her daughter. Rachel recognizes that her mother is frightened: "She's wondering — *what will become of me?"* (114). She realizes that her mother is vulnerable too, especially to mortality. Maybe that's all that her harping on youthful appearances was: a desperate effort to stave off old age.

Rachel finally liberates herself from the symbiotic power play when she realizes that her mother really is under sentence of death but that she, Rachel, can do nothing about it: ". . . I really wonder now why I have been so ruthlessly careful of her, as though to preserve her throughout eternity, a dried flower under glass. It isn't up to me. It never was. I can take care, but only some. I'm not responsible for keeping her alive. There is, suddenly, some enormous relief in this realization" (195). Finally mother and daughter exchange roles — as all parents and children must eventually do — when Rachel realizes, "I am the mother now" (196), as she cares for her "elderly child" (201).

### Niall Cameron

The mortician is the mystery-man of *A Jest of God*. Niall Cameron is Rachel's disappearing father who died long ago. The king of the dead who haunts Rachel's dreams, he holds the clues to Rachel's living death: "He is behind the door I cannot open. And his voice — his voice — so I know he is lying there among them, lying in state, king over them" (19). His is the heart beating beneath the floor, as in Edgar Allan Poe's story, "The Tell-tale Heart." In order to liberate her own identity, Rachel must quest her father in his own realm, the kingdom of the dead. After she has laid him to rest, she may be free to live.

Rachel must collect clues to discover the secret of the puzzle. The first clue to his character is in the Great War: Rachel unearths among her mother's relics "one picture of Niall Cameron, awkwardly proud and unbelievably young in his new uniform as Private in the Artillery in 1915" (99), although Rachel recalls that he would never march with the World War I veterans on Armistice Day. When the Second War came, the Cameron Highlanders marched through Manawaka to the pipes playing "The March of the Cameron Men," but Niall Cameron refused to see the Cameron men off, although they bore his name, merely observing, "It has a fine sound, the lies the pipes tell" (57). Even though he survived the war, something was killed in him, for he returned a dead man who was more comfortable with the corpses downstairs than with his own flesh and blood upstairs.

Niall Cameron also refused to accompany his wife to church: perhaps the Great War destroyed his faith in a benevolent Providence. "Immortality would have appalled him, perhaps as much as it does me" (41), Rachel surmises. Instead, he simply seeks oblivion in alcohol, as Rachel seeks it in sleep or suicide, drinking away his life in the mortuary where she must seek clues to his death.

Questing her father amid the green bottles that house the spirits in the mortuary downstairs where she was never allowed as a child, Rachel discovers, "there's nothing left from then, nothing of him, not a clue" (123) — not even in the olive-green leather book stamped with the scarlet letter A (for accounts, not for adultery) "like the roll of Judgement" (120).

Rachel is finally able to lay her father's ghost and liberate herself from his deadly grip when his successor, Hector Jonas, teaches her that her father chose his own life, as she must choose hers. Rachel learns to respect her parents' mysteries: "their mysteries remain theirs. I don't need to know. . . . I have my own" (198).

### Stacey Cameron MacAindra

The other member of Rachel's family who is absent from *A Jest of God* in the flesh, if not in the spirit, is her sister Stacey, who escaped the manacles of Manawaka long ago to live in Vancouver with her encyclopaedia-salesman husband, Clifford MacAindra, and their brood of four children. Rachel envies Stacey her survival instinct and determined independence: "She knew right from the start what she wanted most, which was to get as far away from Manawaka as possible" (11).

The two sisters could not be more different in personality and situation — opposing personae of the author perhaps, or an exercise in the road not taken. Rachel envies Stacey her husband and children and, even more, her insouciance: "It's all right for Stacey. She'd laugh, probably. Everything is all right for her, easy and open. She doesn't appreciate what she's got. She doesn't even know she's got it. She thinks she's hard done by, for the work caused by four kids and a man who admits her existence. She doesn't have the faintest notion" (99). The grass always looks greener on the other side of the Rockies.

There are two sides to every story, though, and Stacey's side of the story is expressed in Laurence's subsequent novel *The Fire-Dwellers* (1969), where we see Stacey envying Rachel for her peaceful, uncomplicated life. But Stacey also pities Rachel for her land-locked existence, recalling how she left Manawaka herself as a young woman: "Goodbye Prairies. Goodbye to Stacey's sister, always so clever. When I think you're still there I can't bear it" (8). Reading both sisters' stories, we realize that life is never as easy for other people as it appears to us from outside. Laurence's sister novels take us inside the characters so that we know how it feels to be someone else. Eventually the two sisters learn to sympathize with each other, and by the end of each novel, they are en route to reunion, as Rachel sets off for Vancouver with their aging mother at the conclusion of *A Jest of God*.

### Nick Kazlik

Another mystery man, Rachel's lover Nick Kazlik "had his own demons and webs" (189), Rachel realizes. But since we see Nick primarily through Rachel's eyes, we do not know precisely what those demons and webs are. The facts that emerge through the realistic dialogue that Rachel reports, however, give the reader clues that form an ironic counterpoint to Rachel's misinterpretations. Rachel's opposite in most ways, Nick also parallels Rachel in others. Another native of Manawaka, Nick Kazlik comes from the other side of town from Rachel, the *wrong* side of the tracks. A member of one of the Ukrainian families that constitute a contrast to the Waspish Scots-Presbyterians represented by the Camerons, Nick was envied as a boy by Rachel for being "more free" and having more fun: "Not so boxed-in, maybe. More outspoken. More able to speak out" — "Laying girls and doing gay Slavic dances" (87–88), jokes Nick with his "voice's never-quite-caught mockery" (183). Nick seems exotic to Rachel, with his Slavic slanting eyes and mysterious life as a high-school teacher in Winnipeg.

The son of "Nestor the Jester," the town milkman, Nick also felt he was a figure of fun, like Rachel as daughter of the town undertaker — "the milkman's son" and "the undertaker's daughter" (67). Nestor Kazlik has built up a dairy farm and wants to leave his dairy farm to his son, but, unlike his brother, Nick rejects his heritage — an "historical irony," Nick observes (102). Like Rachel, Nick has trouble accepting his inheritance. He quotes the prophet Jeremiah: *"I have forsaken my house — I have left mine heritage — mine heritage is unto me as a lion in the forest — it crieth out against me — therefore have I hated it"* (110).

Like Rachel, Nick also had a sibling — his twin brother Stefan (or Steve). As boys, both brothers had polio, leaving Nick with slightly twisted spine, the kiss of death. But it was Steve who was laid out in his coffin by Rachel's father, the town undertaker — bequeathing to his brother a lifetime of guilt. In his dotage, Nestor calls Nick Steve, the name of the son who wanted to inherit the dairy farm. The snapshot Nick shows Rachel to terminate their relationship, which she assumes is a picture of his son, may be a photograph of Nick's lost boyhood self or his phantom twin (149). Nick's mysteries remain for Rachel and for the reader.

Like Rachel's sister Stacey, Nick escaped Manawaka for college and a career in Winnipeg. But, as Rachel eventually learns, Nick has never married (189) or had children — evidence of those mysterious demons and webs that Rachel can only imagine. Afraid of commitment, Nick has merely amused himself with Rachel while he is home in Manawaka to visit his parents for the summer. Then he escaped to his urban independence when Rachel's expectations (and his parents') became too demanding. Nick Kazlik has a catalytic effect on Rachel's character development, however, as we shall see in the discussion of themes and structures.

## Minor Characters

Three minor characters are significant to the central themes of *A Jest of God*: James Doherty is central to the theme of communication, revealing Rachel's frustrated maternal instincts; Calla Mackie represents the theme of religion, introducing Rachel to the Tabernacle of the Risen and Reborn and the phenomenon of glossalalia; and Hector Jonas, the undertaker, is central to the theme of death, helping Rachel to lay her father's ghost. They inhabit central settings in the novel — James the school, Calla the church, and Hector the mortuary.

## James Doherty

James Doherty plays a small but significant part in the novel. Rachel's favourite pupil, her "teacher's pet," he reveals Rachel's emotional vulnerability. "James, space venturer, first man on the moon" (53), the creator of *splendid* spaceships, where astronauts ascend ropes "like angels climbing Jacob's ladder" (6), appeals to Rachel because the russet-haired, blue-eyed, sparrow-quick boy is so "unique" (3). James also reveals Rachel's paranoia, for she fears that if the class discovered how "I care about James" (25), "They would torment me," and "James would be cruel" — "That's what stings the most" (6).

Rachel's surrogate, James escapes from the prison of the school to wander in the Wachakwa River Valley while he is recuperating from tonsillitis — as Rachel wishes to do. Rachel defends James when the principal accuses him of playing hookey. But when Willard Siddley straps James, Rachel feels she has betrayed the boy (25). Interviewing Grace Doherty about James's absenteeism, Rachel feels jealous of his mother's right to touch him with tenderness (50).

James reveals Rachel's frustrated maternal instincts when her repressed emotions erupt. When James refuses to reveal his paper, Rachel (mistakenly) suspects that he is hiding a cruel caricature of her, proving that "He hates me. I am the enemy" (52). Hurt and humiliated, she lashes out at him, striking him across the face with her ruler, her badge of rule, causing a river of blood to stream down his face, emblem of emotion (52). Fearing that an apology will reveal her vulnerability, causing the children to fall upon her "like falcons," Rachel is unable to utter her silent apology aloud: *"James — I'm sorry"* (53). So Rachel remains both remorseful and shaken by her involuntary violence (54).

## Calla Mackie

Calla Mackie is Rachel's closest friend and perfect foil. With her vibrant smocks and vivid walls, the extroverted Calla is the opposite to the introverted Rachel. Named by her mother for the calla lily symbolizing death, Calla is more like "a sunflower, if anything, brash, strong, plain, and yet reaching up in some way" (9). Calla introduces the theme of rebirth by giving Rachel a "hyacinth, bulbously in bud and just about to give birth to the blue-purple blossom" (9).

Calla has much to teach Rachel: she introduces Rachel to the Tabernacle of the Risen and Reborn, where Rachel is given "the gift of tongues" (26). Calla also teaches Rachel Saint Paul's dictum, *"If any man among you thinketh himself to be wise, let him become a fool, that he may be wise"* (135) — another important lesson that Rachel has to learn. Calla also shows Rachel her mute songbird, for she tries to teach Rachel, as well as Jacob, to sing. Singing *"She's Only a Bird in a Gilded Cage"* (47), Calla tries to liberate Rachel from her prison of solipsism and show her the angel at the top of her ladder (137).

Calla's love for Rachel outlasts Nick's. Although initially Rachel is repelled by Calla's kiss after her outburst in the Tabernacle, eventually Rachel realizes, "the truth is that she loves me" (198). Although Rachel sometimes resents Calla's intrusiveness, she appreciates her for being "kind and well-meaning" (3). When Rachel believes she is pregnant, the person she turns to is Calla, because she realizes that there is "Only one person" (173) who can help. Calla's response to Rachel's cry for help is to offer to drop everything to help Rachel in her moment of need. She responds reassuringly, "We could manage. As for the baby, well, my Lord, I've looked after many a kid before" (175).

When Rachel says goodbye to Calla before leaving Manawaka, Calla is generous enough to say, referring to Rachel's false pregnancy, "I'm sorry that things weren't different for you" (197). But Rachel has also learned to be generous enough to respond, "I'm sorry that things weren't different for you. I mean, that I wasn't different" (198). "Calla, pillar of tabernacles, speaker in tongues, mother of canaries and budgerigars," replies, "Not to worry, . . . I'll survive"

(198). Laurence wrote that her major theme is "survival, the attempt of the personality to survive with some dignity" ("Ten" 21). Calla teaches Rachel survival skills. "Bold as brass and twice as loud," Calla also teaches Rachel to shout *"Hallelujah"* (135), so that Rachel can finally sing her own ode to joy (202).

## Hector Jonas

Hector Jonas, like Calla Mackie, is a crucial though minor character. Hector is the mortician who has replaced Rachel's father as the proprietor of the undertaking parlour downstairs. Although he "has for so long plied his trade below while I tried to live above" (124), Rachel realizes she hardly knows him. Nevertheless, when she is in the depths of despair, it is to Hector she appeals. For the first time in the novel, Rachel really says what she thinks when she asks Hector, "Let me come in," and thinks, "That was my voice? That prideless-ness?" (119). Equally important, when she leaves the mortuary, she begins, automatically, to apologize, as usual. But this time she stops herself, thinking, "Go on, Rachel. Apologize. Go on apologizing for ever, go on until nothing of you is left. Is that what you want the most?" Instead, she replaces apology with appreciation, saying, "No — listen, Hector — what I mean is, thanks" (128).

Hector's name is significant: Jonas inevitably recalls the Biblical parable of Jonah in the belly of the whale, the parallel for Rachel trapped in the tomb of her living death suggested in the epigraph to the novel. The name Hector links him ironically with the warrior Prince Hector, son of King Priam of Troy, who was killed in combat by Achilles.

A grotesque comic figure, with his short legs and red suspenders, jumping off the mortuary table "like a small stout athlete from a trampoline" (125), Hector is actually a wise man. "Comic prophet, dwarf seer" (124), perched on his altar of death, Hector answers the riddle of the Sphinx when he helps Rachel to understand her father and to come to terms with his death.

Ruler of this burlesque Hades, complete with wrought-iron staves like "Ye Olde Dungeon" (118), Hector is a Pluto figure, king of the dead. Hector helps Rachel lay her father's ghost, as together they hold a wake, singing saccharine hymns, drinking rye spirits, and weeping real tears in the grand old tradition. Following this ritual libation,

Hector leads Rachel, a Persephone figure, as his bride up the aisle of death. Following this parody ritual resurrection, Rachel is ready to return to reality and climb the stairs out of Hades back to life.

Under all this weight of symbolism and allegory, however, Hector turns out (naturally enough) to be a real human being, just like Rachel. When she weeps in response to his song and his sympathy, Hector shares his own sore point (or Achilles's heel) with her: "At the crucial moment, my wife laughs. She says she can't help it — I look funny" (127–28). Suddenly, Rachel sees him "living there behind his eyes" (128) — the same eyes that moments before appeared "lynx eyes, cat's eyes, the green slanted cat's eyes of glass marbles" (124) — like the glass cat's eyes in her death dream. Finally, Rachel has realized that other people are real — perhaps the most important lesson that experience (or fiction) can teach us.

### Lee Toy

Other minor characters are either parallels to Rachel, like Lee Toy, or threats to her survival, like Willard Siddley. Lee Toy, the solitary Chinese man, lives in secrecy alone above the Regal Café, just as Rachel lives in silence over the Japonica Funeral Parlour. Symbolized by the "solitary and splendidly plumaged tiger" (55) of his wall painting, Lee Toy parallels Rachel's isolation.

### Nestor Kazlik

Nick Kazlik's father, "Nestor the Jester" (188), named for the father of Ulysses, also parallels Rachel in surprising ways. A "great bear of a man, with a moustache thick as an untrimmed hedge" (69), his strong Slavic face "high-cheekboned as a Cree's" (187), he seems Rachel's opposite, as Rachel recalls how the jovial Manawaka milkman used to give the children rides on his sleigh. Like Rachel, however, "He makes a kind of theatre out of his life" (146), "creating the world in his own image" (142), and looking "as though the rest of the world were an interesting but unlikely story he had once told himself" (187). Guarded now by his wife Teresa, "a low stone tower of a woman" (187), the aging, senile Nestor Kazlik also lives in the dead past, calling Nick by the name of his dead twin Steve and giving Rachel a greeting for her dead father. Refusing to acknowledge facts and stubbornly imposing his internal world on external reality, Nestor intends to leave his dairy farm to the son who rejects it. Since Rachel has recovered from her isolation, she can sympathize with Nestor's solipsism.

## Willard Siddley

Willard Siddley, sadistic school principal, on the other hand, appears to Rachel as a threat. His very name suggests a sinister figure. She visualizes him as a dangerous animal — a vulture (23) or reptile (45). Rachel suspects him of being a sadist, since he "likes using the strap on boys" (7). His "spotted furry hands" (9) both attract and repel her, because "With them he touches his wife, and holds the strap to strike a child, and — " (44). She also perceives his eyes as hostile and hypnotic behind his thick glasses: "His eyes are pallid, like the blue dead eyes of the frozen whitefish" (7). But when she gains confidence, she sees his eyes are vulnerable behind his thick glasses, soliciting her affection (43): "his whitefish eyes, hoping for some slight friendliness from me, possibly, while I sit here conjuring up dragons to scare myself with" (157). Rather than threatening her, Rachel realizes that he might just have found her attractive and hoped for "admiration or reassurance" (157).

## Rachel's Suitors

Rachel's other suitors are significant too, although they are even more shadowy than Nick Kazlik. Rachel recalls with chagrin the salesman in embalming fluid who took her to the Regal Café for dinner and admired her for her "good bones" (16–17). Even more embarrassing was the town clown, Cluny Macpherson from the B.A. Garage: "short and broad, like a bulldog," he used to get a kick out of clowning on the floor of the Flamingo Dancehall with the adolescent Rachel, who was like a "skinny poplar sapling," humiliating her even more than himself (60–61). A more serious suitor was Lennox Cates, who asked Rachel out when she came home to Manawaka from university in Winnipeg. When he started asking her out twice a week, she stopped seeing him before it went any further, because she could not visualize herself as the wife of a farmer, a man who never even finished high school. When she recalls teaching three of his children, all nice-looking and fair-haired like Lennox, she questions her own prejudices (31).

## Chorus of Clowns

Rachel sees other characters as clowns, from "Nestor the Jester," a "giant buffoon" (188), to Cluny Macpherson, who "liked being a clown" (61), to the stiffs downstairs "powdered whitely like clowns" (19), to the "brutal joker" (42), God Himself. The rest of the world, especially her former pupils, form a kind of Greek chorus commenting on the tragedy of Rachel's life — "an unseen audience ready to hoot and caw with a shocking derision" (95) — chanting "like a Greek chorus . . . *Dead, dead, dead*" (107). But Rachel will revive.

### THEMES: "SURVIVING WITH DIGNITY"

The major themes of *A Jest of God* — death, religion, love, communication, and identity — create a continuum of ideas. Laurence wrote that her earliest theme was "the promised land of one's own inner freedom." But as she matured as a writer, she discovered that "the theme had changed to that of survival, the attempt of the personality to survive with some dignity, toting the load of excess mental baggage that everyone carries, until the moment of death" ("Ten" 21).

## Death: "The Skull beneath the Skin"

Because Margaret Laurence experienced the loss of so many loved ones in her life, beginning with the death of both parents when she was just a young child, she is naturally preoccupied with mortality. Death is a central theme in all of her novels, especially *A Jest of God*, and each of her heroines must come to terms with her own mortality. Laurence is anything but morbid, however, and her fiction is far from deadly. Rather, she believes that acknowledging death is essential to appreciate life, and each of her flawed protagonists must die figuratively to be reborn as complete individuals. The characters must also come to terms with the past, often in the form of deceased ancestors, before they can survive the present and face the future.

Laurence juxtaposes life and death throughout *A Jest of God*, because they are inextricably connected, two sides of the same coin. The hillside where Rachel gathers crocuses in early spring is "just beyond the cemetery" (79). And when Nick tries to persuade Rachel to make love with him on the banks of the Wachakwa River, he reassures her, "it's as private as the grave" (90). Rachel's friend Calla, named for the lily that is a symbol of death, initiates the theme of rebirth by giving Rachel "A hyacinth, bulbously in bud and just about to give birth to the blue-purple blossom" (9).

"Death's unmentionable" (122) in polite society, Rachel says, and so death is not allowed across the tracks that divide upper-class Manawaka from lower-class: "No one in Manawaka ever dies, at least not on this side of the tracks. We are a gathering of immortals. We pass on, through Calla's divine gates of topaz and azure, perhaps, but we do not die. Death is rude, unmannerly, not to be spoken to in the street" (13). But when Rachel attempts "a denial of death," trying to ignore "The skull beneath the skin" (122), Hector Jonas replies, "Who can deny it? . . . It happens" (121). "The undertaker's daughter" (67), Rachel can hardly deny death, since she lives above a funeral parlour in the ironically named "Cameron Funeral Home," with a sign out front advertising the mortuary. Niall Cameron's sign said "Cameron's Funeral Parlour" in black lettering on a pale-grey background, but Hector's blue neon sign flashes "Japonica Funeral Chapel," like a night club. Rachel reflects, "All that remains is for someone to delete the word *funeral*. A nasty word, smacking of mortality" (13).

No wonder Rachel is so adamant about denying death *and* so fascinated by it. Because her father is deceased, Rachel is haunted by mortality. Many of the novel's motifs are buried in her nightmare of the kingdom of death: "The stairs descending to the place where I am not allowed. The giant bottles and jars stand there, bubbled green glass. The silent people are there, lipsticked and rouged, powdered whitely like clowns. How funny they look, each lying dressed in best, and their open eyes are glass eyes, cat's eye marbles, round glass beads, blue and milky, unwinking" (19).

Rachel's dead father is the mystery man of *A Jest of God*, as we have seen. "He is behind the door I cannot open. And his voice — his voice

— so I know he is lying there among them, lying in state, king over them" (19). *A Jest of God* is a murder-mystery, and the crucial question is "Who killed Niall Cameron?" To free herself for life, Rachel must solve the mystery of her father's death. The answer to the question "Who will bury the undertaker" is "Whoever will undertake it." Like Hamlet, Rachel must undertake to lay her father's ghost.

Like Jonah, Rachel has been "swallowed deep in the dark," for the death of her father virtually killed her too. When he died, Rachel had to come back home to Manawaka from college in Winnipeg: "I couldn't finish university after Dad's death. The money wasn't there" (11). When her mother covered the furniture with lace doilies, Rachel thought it was so that death would not rub off on their home (16). And when her mother said that "Your father's not feeling well" — meaning he was drunk — Rachel thought she meant he had caught the germ of death. Finally he succumbs, and Rachel catches the germ of death from him. So Rachel's adult life ended with her father's, and she has been playing dead ever since to compete with the corpses and win the approval of the mortician.

Rachel is a walking zombie at the beginning of the novel. Reflections in mirrors suggest a ghost: "a thin streak of a person, like the stroke of a white chalk on a blackboard," "like the negative of a photograph" (29). "I can see myself in the mirror, not quite see but almost, the silver fishwhite of arms, the crane of a body, gaunt metal or gaunt bird" (115). Rachel is so "bone-thin" that underwater her "cross of bones" looks like the skeleton of a drowned body (139). Calla says that Rachel looks "like death warmed over" (174), and Rachel is surprised that real blood runs in her veins, instead of embalming fluid (117). No wonder one suitor, a travelling salesman in embalming fluid, admired her for her "good bones" (17), like an Egyptian mummy.

Niall Cameron died long before they buried him: he drank his life away downstairs in the mortuary, replacing the blood in his veins with the embalming fluid of alcohol — just like a mortician. As a child, Rachel was hurt because her father preferred to stay down in the mortuary with the corpses, rather than upstairs with his family. She was jealous of the dead who claimed her father's attention — children like Nick Kazlik's brother Steve. So Rachel must discover the secret of "the place where I am not allowed" (19): "This is no place for you, Rachel" (118), her father always said: "run away Rachel run away" (19).

Only after she has come to life with Nick does Rachel have the courage to descend to that forbidden nightmare place to search for clues to the mysterious disappearance of her father. Descending the dream stairs, with their faded flowered carpeting of "trampled roses," is like descending into the underworld, down the primrose path to hell. The scrolls of wrought-iron on the huge door make it appear like a cartoon version of "Ye Olde Dungeon" (118), and Hector Jonas, the new mortician, is a "Comic prophet, dwarf seer" (124) — a Pluto figure, or grotesque god of death presiding over this synthetic Hades.

So desperate is Rachel to find her father that she actually says what she thinks for the very first time in the novel, when she demands that Hector open the door (119). Speech distinguishes the living from the "unspeaking" dead (13). So Rachel's confrontation with death is already bringing her to life.

Rachel searches for clues in the green glass bottles (bottles for spirits), but they contain no scrawled message from the marooned man. Even the olive leather book with the scarlet latter A for Accounts, "like the roll of Judgement" (120), cannot account for his disappearance. "Nothing is as it used to be, and there's nothing left from then, nothing of him, not a clue" (123). In her bewilderment, she turns to Hector to ask, "Why do you think he stayed, Hector? *Did he like them?*" (123). Hector's reply is critical: "I would bet he had the kind of life he wanted most" (124). Rachel realizes, *"The life he wanted most.* If my father had wanted otherwise, it would have been otherwise. Not necessarily better, but at least different. Did he ever try to alter it? Did I, with mine? Was that what he needed most, after all, not ever to have to touch any living thing? Was that why she came to life after he died?" (124–25).

This constitutes the turning point of the novel, because Rachel realizes that she cannot control her father's (or mother's) life or death, but she *can* control her own. So, if she does not like her life, she can and must change it. Thus, she exorcises her father's ghost and her own shade. Later she realizes, "He probably did do what he wanted most, even though he might not have shown it. But maybe what came of it was something he hadn't bargained for" (199). On her final visit to the mortuary to say farewell to Hector Jonas, Rachel recalls,

47

The last time I was in the Japonica Funeral Chapel was that night I came down here late and talked to Hector. Everything looks just the same, but now it does not seem to matter much that my father's presence has been gone from here for a long time. I can't know what he was like. He isn't here to say, and even if he were, he wouldn't say, any more than Mother does. Whatever it was that happened with either of them, their mysteries remain theirs. I don't need to know. It isn't necessary. I have my own. (198)

Once she has laid her father's ghost to rest, Rachel returns to life. Her rebirth is celebrated ritualistically: Hector Jonas escorts her through his chapel of death, "leading me like a bride up the aisle" (125) and back to life in a grotesque parody of a ritual rebirth. If Rachel is a Persephone figure and Hector is Hades, her shadowy consort, Rachel's mother is still above ground, like Demeter or Ceres, summoning her daughter back to life. Rachel's period as queen of the dead is over, and now she must return to the land of the living to be *"queen of the golden city"* (1).

Revival requires emotion — both tears and laughter. Rachel shows signs of life by beginning to develop a sense of humour: when Hector announces, "I got a really super-dooper automatic organ," Rachel is tempted to tell him "a joke about an angel who traded his harp for an upright organ" (126). Hector plays a hymn on his organ for Rachel, as they sit on "the mourner's bench" and drink and weep, holding a wake for Niall Cameron in "the chapel purged of all spirit, all spirits except the rye" (127). Hector plays a hymn for Rachel — not Bach's grave chorale "Jesu Joy of Man's Desiring" appropriate for "[t]he carriage trade" (126), but a sentimental song about saints and angels (127) — making Rachel weep for the first time. As she waters her father's grave with her tears, her libation is also a life-giving rain for Rachel — as crucial an outburst as her cry during her first orgasm with Nick — for after the wake, Rachel awakes.

Seeing her emotion, Hector sympathizes and responds to her outburst by revealing his own sore spot — or Achilles' heel: "At the crucial moment, my wife laughs. She says she can't help it — I look funny" (127–28). This revelation prompts Rachel to see another human being from inside for the very first time. Before, "Hector's eyes are lynx eyes, cat's eyes, the green slanted cat's eyes of glass marbles" (124) — like the glass eyes of the corpses in her nightmare

(19) — but now, "I look into his face then, and for an instant see him living there behind his eyes" (128). She even learns to stop apologizing for living: as she is about to go back upstairs, she begins, "I'm — look, I'm sorry I came down, Hector. I don't know why — I don't know what I was thinking of — " (128). Thinking, "Go on, Rachel. Apologize. Go on apologizing for ever, go on until nothing of you is left. Is that what you want the most?" she changes her tune: "No — listen, Hector — what I mean is, thanks" (128). Having faced death, Rachel can now turn and climb the stairs back to life.

Like Calla, Rachel can say, "I'll survive" (198). And like Jonah, Rachel "came out alive after all." Laurence wrote, "The theme of survival — not just physical survival, but the preservation of some human dignity and in the end some human warmth and ability to reach out and touch others" is central to all her work (*Heart* 6). Rachel survives with dignity and humanity.

### Religion: "The Brutal Joker"

The title of the novel *A Jest of God* is our first clue to the central theme of religion. Church is the normal setting for religion, and Laurence presents two churches in the first three chapters of the novel. When she returned home to Manawaka from university in Winnipeg upon the death of her father, Rachel refused to go to church on the grounds that "God hadn't died recently, within the last few years, but a long time ago, longer than I could remember, for I could not actually recall a time when He was alive" (39). Her father refused to go to church too, preferring to tend his corpses "in the conviction that they'd found by now all there was — oblivion," and eventually Niall Cameron also finds oblivion. "Immortality would have appalled him, perhaps as much as it does me" (41), Rachel concludes. So perhaps God the Father died when Rachel's father did.

Soon, however, Rachel demonstrates her reversion to childhood by accompanying her mother to church, even though she still believes that she does not believe. Hearing old Tom Gillanders sing "Jerusalem the Golden," Rachel thinks, "If I believed, I would have to detest God for the brutal joker He would be if He existed" (42). Little does Rachel realize how right she is. She accompanies her mother because "Going to church is a social occasion for her" (39): "She loves coming to church because she sees everyone, and in spring the new hats are like a forest of tulips. But as for faith — I suppose she takes it for granted that she believes. Yet if the Reverend MacElfrish should suddenly lose his mind and speak of God with anguish or joy, or out of some need should pray with fierce humility as though God had to be there, Mother would be shocked to the core. Luckily, it will never happen" (41). Rachel reflects cynically, "as for anyone speaking in a clarion voice about their beliefs — it seems indecent to her, almost in the same class as what she calls foul language" (26).

Calla Mackie is at the core of the theme of religion, just as Hector Jonas was at the heart of the theme of death (two closely related themes), because Calla takes Rachel to the Tabernacle where her first religious experience takes place. Calla's church, the *"Tabernacle of the Risen and Reborn"* (29) — its name suggesting the theme of resurrection and rebirth — is the opposite of the Camerons' proper Presbyterian Church. The portraits of Jesus illustrate the contrast: the Tabernacle portrays a virile, suffering Christ, "bearded and bleeding, his heart exposed and bristling with thorns like a scarlet pincushion" (30), while the "stained-glass window [of the Presbyterian Church] shows a pretty and clean-cut Jesus expiring gently and with absolutely no inconvenience, no gore, no pain, just this nice and slightly effeminate insurance salesman" (41).

The decor is the opposite too: the woodwork of the Presbyterian Church is "beautifully finished. Nothing ornate — heaven forbid" (41), whereas the Tabernacle boasts a pulpit "bulky and new, pale wood blossoming in bunches of grapes and small sharp birds with beaks uplifted" (30) in a celebration of God's creation. The outside of the building that houses the Tabernacle is fanciful too, with pillars and turrets, glassed-in porches and wrought-iron balconies, and, most significant of all, "the blue and red glass circle of a rose-window at the very top" (29), emblem of love. Whereas the Bible in the Presbyterian Church is black as death, the Tabernacle's Bible — which the preacher calls "The Book of Life, The Counsel of Heaven, the true words written by Him on High, He the sole Author" (33) — rests on a pulpit draped with white velvet and tasselled with silver threads, the book covered with glittering cloth like gold, looking as if it might glow in the dark or give off sparks (30).

The people are even more different than the place, especially the preachers. "Mr. MacElfrish's voice is as smooth and mellifluous as always, and he is careful not to say anything which might be upsetting. His sermon deals with Gratitude. He says we are fortunate to be living here, in plenty [Manitoba means God's plenty], and we ought not to take our blessings for granted. Who is likely to quibble with that?" (41). The lay preacher at the Tabernacle, however, stretches out his arms to captivate his congregation, making the Bible sound like a Technicolor movie, a religious epic (33), as he urges them to receive the gift of tongues and to participate "in the joy felt and known by any one of our brothers or sisters as they experience that deep and private enjoyment, that sublime edification, the infilling of the Spirit" (34).

The hymns are a good example of the vast difference in these two forms of worship — one deeply felt, the other bleached clean of feeling. The Presbyterian hymns are proper, the church carillon ringing out *"The Church's One Foundation"* (40) in celebration of the ecclesiastical establishment, and the soloist singing *"Jerusalem the Golden"* (42). The Tabernacle's hymns are harrowing, however:

> *Day of wrath! O day of mourning!*
> *See fulfilled the prophet's warning!*
> *Heaven and earth in ashes burning!* (32)

The exclamation marks emphasize the excitement of the hymn's annunciation of Judgement Day. Rachel feels threatened by this hymn "macabre as the messengers of the apocalypse, the gaunt horsemen, the cloaked skeletons I dreamed of once when I was quite young" (32). The next hymn expresses the singer's surrender to the coming of Christ in terms that are almost sexual:

> *In full and glad surrender,*
> *I give myself to Thee,*
> *Thine utterly and only*
> *And evermore to be.* (34)

The last hymn celebrates the joy of the marriage of Christ to his Church:

> *Rejoice! Rejoice! Emmanuel*
> *Shall come to thee, O Israel!* (35)

The Tabernacle is a paragon of passion compared to the sober Presbyterian Church.

Most threatening of all to Rachel is the congregation of the Tabernacle, where one parishioner stands up and testifies, like "the chanting of some mad enchanter, himself enchanted" (35), while the man seated next to her moans with feeling, shocking Rachel with the openness of the sound. The Presbyterian congregation, in contrast, appear to view church as a social club where they can gossip and show off their new clothes to their friends.

Calla has warned Rachel that "the gift of tongues" has been granted to the congregation of the Tabernacle. The preacher quotes Saint Paul's first epistle to the Corinthians, 12.4–10: *"Now there are diversities of gifts, but the same Spirit. For to one is given by the Spirit the word of wisdom — to another the word of knowledge — to another the gifts of healing — to another prophecy — to another divers kinds of tongues — "* (33). Calla says, "We hold ourselves too tightly these days, that's the trouble. Afraid to let the Spirit speak through us" (26–27). She explains that Saint Paul says, *"I thank my God I speak with tongues more than ye all.* And what about *the tongues of men and of angels?* What else does the tongues of angels mean, it not glossalalia?" (27).

Glossalalia, the gift of tongues or ecstatic utterances, is a religious ecstasy in which the speaker, inspired by the Holy Spirit, speaks involuntarily, even unconsciously, perhaps without understanding what he is saying, although another listener may be able to interpret. Ecstasy means to stand outside, and the ancient Greeks believed that in a state of ecstasy the soul left the body. There are three forms of ecstasy: religious, sexual, and artistic. Ancient and mediaeval peoples were not as careful as modern cultures to distinguish between these various kinds of rapture, and Laurence suggests their close relationships, for "there are diversities of gifts, but the same Spirit." Rachel's outcry in the Tabernacle echoes her outburst in school with James Doherty and prefigures her orgasmic cry of Nick's name when they make love.

The Bacchae, worshippers of Dionysus, the Greek god of erotic love, were a cult that cultivated ecstasy, working themselves into a frenzy that might involve cannibalistic rites, tearing to pieces and eating a young male victim to symbolize devouring the god of love himself. Rachel associates the Tabernacle's glossalalia with the Bacchantes: "Celebrate confusion. Let us celebrate confusion. God is not the author of confusion but of peace. What a laugh. Let the

Dionysian women rend themselves on the night hills and consume the god" (36).

Rachel is apprehensive that Calla may stand and speak: "Will there be ecstatic utterances and will Calla suddenly rise and keen like the Grecian women wild on the hills, or wail in a wolf's voice, or speak as hissingly as a cell of serpents?" (31). She is appalled when a young man stands, his eyes closed, "like a blind seer, a younger Tiresias come to tell the king the words that no one could listen to and live": "*Galamani halafaka tabinota caragoya lal lal ufranti*" (35). Rachel is terrified that Calla will rise and testify:

> *That voice!*
> Chattering, crying, ululating, the forbidden transformed cryptically to nonsense, dragged from the crypt, stolen and shouted, the shuddering of it, the fear, the breaking, the release, the grieving —
> Not Calla's voice. Mine. Oh my God. Mine. The voice of Rachel. (36)

The voice of Rachel is mourning for her lost children, like her biblical namesake. Here we hear the outcry of both Rachel's spirit and body, her need for both spiritual and sexual love erupting after a lifetime of repression.

But Rachel rejects this knowledge and dismisses her outburst as hysteria. She also rejects Calla's offer of comfort and love, recoiling in revulsion from Calla's kiss. Rachel has not yet learned Laurence's belief in compassion. Saint Paul reminds us: "Though I speak with the tongues of men and of angels, and have not charity, I am become as sounding brass, or a tinkling cymbal" (1 Corinthians 13.1). Clearly Rachel still has a lot to learn.

There is a second instalment to the gift of tongues, however. When Rachel returns to visit Calla in chapter 8, Calla informs Rachel that she has reread Saint Paul and recognized his caution: "*There are, it may be, so many kinds of voices in the world, and none of them is without signification. Therefore if I know not the meaning of the voice, I shall be unto him that speaketh a barbarian, and he that speaketh shall be a barbarian unto me*" (135). Rachel considers "the apostle's appallingly accurate sight" (135) as "God's irony — that we should for so long believe it is only the few who speak in tongues" (134).

God's gift of tongues is not to be confused with the Tower of Babel, symbol of the failure of communication. The preacher reminds the congregation that Paul said, *"God is not the author of confusion but of peace, as in all the churches of the saints"* (33), and Calla praised "the peace the person who's been gifted comes back with" (27). Calla announces to Rachel that she has been given the gift of tongues and spoken alone in her own home, saying, "It was peace. Like some very gentle falling of rain" (136) — peace, not confusion — like the peace and pride Rachel feels after making love with Nick (91). Calla also recalls that Paul cautioned, *"If any man among you thinketh himself to be wise, let him become a fool, that he may be wise"* (135) — prophetic words for Rachel.

Rachel continues to deny God, however, even after this religious experience, although she also continues to pray to a God in whom she claims not to believe: "I don't know why a person pleads with God. If I believed, the last kind of a Creator I could imagine would be a human-type Being who could be reached by tears or bribed with words. *Say please, Rachel, it's the magic word.* Mother. Please, God, let him phone" (95). Rachel's love affair with Nick brings her closer to God. Recalling her virgin awkwardness, she prays, "All right, God — go ahead and laugh, and I'll laugh with you, but not quite yet for a while" (115). After Nick rejects her, Rachel realizes that her situation could be seen as "a joke if viewed from the outside." Her reaction to this perspective is to castigate God: "This I could argue with You (if You were there) until doomsday" (151).

Gradually, Rachel's prayers take on more conviction, and she finally prays in desperation: "I am on my knees. I am not praying — if that is what I am doing — out of belief. Only out of need. Not faith, or belief, or the feeling of deserving anything. None of that seems to be so." She pleads: *"Help me.* Help — if You will — me. Whoever that may be. And whoever You are, or where." She acknowledges, "We seem to have fought for a long time, I and You. The ones who do not have anyone else, turn to You — don't you think I know? All the nuts and oddballs turn to You. Last resort. Don't you think I know?" She laments, "If You have spoken, I am not aware of having heard. If You have a voice, it is not comprehensible to me. No omens. No burning bush, no pillar of sand by day or pillar of flame by night" (171). Nick said, when he rejected Rachel, "I'm not God. I can't solve anything" (148). God does not answer

Rachel, unlike Jonah, but we are taught that God helps them that help themselves, and Rachel does find in prayer the strength to bear her burden, her baby.

When the baby she believes she is incubating turns out to be a tumour, Rachel prays, *"Oh my God. I didn't bargain for this. Not this"* (180). While recuperating from surgery to remove the tumour, she prays, *"Nothing must disturb me"*: "This was all I prayed, to no one or to whoever might be listening, prayed unprayerfully, not with any violence of demand or any valiance of hope, but only sending the words out, in case. *Do you read me?* This message is being sent out to the cosmos, or into the same, by an amateur transmitter who wishes for the moment to sign off. Don't let anything happen. I wasn't quite myself" (185). When Rachel returns to herself, she retrieves responsibility from God: "I quit sending out my swaddled embryo wishes for nothing to happen. No use asking the impossible, even of God" (186). Rachel even responds to her mother's refusal to move on the grounds of her weak heart by saying that God alone knows what is best (195), for she has realized that only God has the power of life and death.

The tumour proves to be not malignant, but benign, like God himself. This is the ultimate jest of God, the means God employs to teach Rachel humility and love of life. Although she does not deliver a child, she does give birth to a new adult self. God makes her a fool so that she can become wise. Through the trial of the false pregnancy and real tumour, Rachel has learned to rejoice in being alive. She thinks, "I do not know how many bones need be broken before I can walk. And I do not know, either, how many need not have been broken at all" (201). She recalls Psalm 51: *"Make me to hear joy and gladness, that the bones which Thou hast broken may rejoice"* (201). Finally Rachel develops a sense of humour, enough to get God's joke and to pity the Joker Himself: "God's mercy on reluctant jesters. God's grace on fools. God's pity on God" (202).

### Communication: *"The Gift of Tongues"*

"The problem of communication is central in Margaret Laurence's novels" (n. pag.), especially in *A Jest of God*, as G.D. Killam points out in his introduction to the novel. Since Rachel is the narrator of this first-person, present-tense novel, the narrative is a form of confession or self-therapy, because Rachel's inability to express herself is both symptom and cause of her neurosis. As Laurence said, "we must attempt to communicate however imperfectly, if we are not to succumb to despair or madness" (*Long* 124–25). *A Jest of God* records Rachel's struggle to save her sanity and survive in a sometimes insane world.

Speech is the faculty that both distinguishes human beings from the other animals and distinguishes the living from the dead, "the unspeaking ones" (13). In *A Jest of God*, silence is a sign of death, speech a sign of life. Rachel's silence is a clue to her moribund nature. Calla's canary Jacob, a silent song-bird, symbolizes the mute Rachel (47), for Rachel has yet to find her tongue. So the mere fact that Rachel is telling her story is positive proof of life.

Laurence wants to help women to find their own voice, to give her heroines "the gift of tongues" (26). But Rachel's voice is stifled in interior monologues. Her only real outcries are silent screams rendered in emphatic italics: *"My God. How can I stand —"* (17). The occasions when Rachel's inner voice surfaces — in the Tabernacle (36), in lovemaking (148), and in grief (181) — are rare but significant. Eventually Rachel's inner and outer voices unite at the turning point of her development, and she can finally speak her mind. Let us look at the way Laurence teaches Rachel to speak and ultimately, to sing.

Rachel shares Laurence's fine ear for language, for the spoken word. "Voice" may be the most often repeated word in *A Jest of God*, appearing dozens of times. Rachel apprehends reality as voices: she recalls hearing the lonely night call of train whistles — "the trainvoice that said *don't stay don't stay just don't every stay — go and keep on going, never mind where.* The mourning and mockery of that voice, like blues. The only lonelier sound I ever heard was the voices of the loons on the spruce-edged lake up at Galloping Mountain. . . . People say *loon*, meaning mad. Crazy as a loon. They were mad, those bird voices" (167–68).

Voice is evidence of identity. Rachel identifies herself as a voice: "I can hear my own voice, eagerly abject" (45). She apprehends other people as voices: characterizing her mother's coven of bridge cronies as "voices. Shrill, sedate, not clownish to their ears but only to mine, and of such unadmitted sadness I can scarcely listen and yet cannot stop listening" (98).

Rachel listens to other people, but does she hear? Her "mother's archaic simper voice" (90) echoes most resonantly in her mind, even in her dreams. She apprehends her dead father only as a disembodied voice: "his voice — his voice — so I know he is lying there among them, lying in state, king over them. He can't fool me." Then, "My mother is singing in a falsetto voice, the stylish tremolo, the ladies' choir voice" (19). Even in her dreams, her mother's voice is false. But so is Rachel's, for she can only speak in artificial voices.

When Rachel does speak out loud, it is in borrowed voices — the "Peter-Rabbitish voice" (4) of a simpering schoolmarm or the "robot's mechanical voice" (48) of the dummy she thinks she is. Rachel is truly a polyphonic narrator: as well-read a woman as her creator, Rachel also speaks in the myriad voices of famous authors, from the Bible, through Shakespeare, Donne, and Marvell, to Wordsworth and Kipling, as we will see in the discussion of allusions. Most insidious of all, she hears in her own words "this echo of my mother's voice" (4), as she speaks in "Mother's voice, lilting and ladylike" (78), revealing how she has internalized her mother's life-denying attitudes: "*A woman's most precious possession.* My mother's archaic simper voice" (89–90) — creating a prison within her own skull that she cannot break out of. Rachel must exorcise her "mother tongue" before she can find her own voice.

Of course Rachel does speak; she just doesn't say what she really thinks. Clearly she has internalized the hypocrisy of society. The actual dialogue that Rachel reports provides an ironic counterpoint with her tacit inner thoughts. She answers her mother's query, "That you, Rachel?" with a simple "Yes," but thinks sarcastically, "Who does she think it is — the Angel of Death?" (94).

Part of the reason that Rachel cannot speak is because she has no one to talk to — except herself, and a God she claims not to believe in. In the section on religion, we saw how often she addressed God, praying deliberately or even involuntarily, unconsciously prefacing her thoughts with the apostrophe, "Oh God!"

The true voice of Rachel first surfaces in the Tabernacle where she is given "the gift of tongues" (26). When Calla Mackie told Rachel that the congregation of the Tabernacle had been given the gift of glossalalia, she said, "We hold ourselves too tightly these days, that's the trouble. Afraid to let the Spirit speak through us" (26–27) — certainly that is Rachel's trouble. Horrified, Rachel hears

*That voice!*

Chattering, crying, ululating, the forbidden transformed cryptically to nonsense, dragged from the crypt, stolen and shouted, the shuddering of it, the fear, the breaking, the release, the grieving — . (36)

So unfamiliar is this "alien voice" (48) that only later does she realize it is "Not Calla's voice. Mine. Oh my God. Mine. The voice of Rachel" (36).

The voice of Rachel is heard mourning for her lost children, like her biblical namesake. Rachel describes the Tabernacle as being like the ocean: "The painted walls are heavy with their greenish blue, not the clear blue of open places but dense and murky, the way the sea must be, fathoms under" (30). The ocean is a symbol for the unconscious, and during the harrowing hymns and passionate sermon, Rachel does descend into the profound depths of her psyche where her oracular voice originates. She also characterizes the Tabernacle as a crypt (31), but this tomb becomes a womb from which Rachel is born.

The birth is abortive, however, because Rachel rejects it as hysteria — from the Greek word for womb (as in "hysterectomy"), suggesting that hysteria is a female disease, resulting from sexual frustration. Certainly this implication would apply to Rachel, for her outburst is the cry of both her spirit and her body demanding both love of God and love of man. It prefigures her outcry in the moment of orgasm when she calls: " 'Nick — *Nick* — ' Only his name. Only, at this moment, his name. The only word" (148). As a result of this breakthrough, Rachel "speaks from faith, not logic" and says, "If I had a child, I would like it to be yours," echoing her namesake's cry, "*Give me my children*" (148). The third and last time the voice of Rachel will issue from the tomb where it has been buried deep in Rachel's psyche is when she learns that the embryo, fruit of her moment of love with Nick, is not a child but a tumour: "My speaking voice, and then only that other voice, wordless and terrible, the voice of some woman mourning for her children" (181).

Even though Nick leaves her and she loses their child, he bequeaths her an invaluable legacy: through his loving, he teaches her to speak. Communication involves listening as well as speaking, and many of their conversations take place on the telephone, the modern-day umbilical chord of communication. Rachel hears many voices, but she does not really listen to what they say. When she says, "Try to listen," and her mother replies, "I've always listened," Rachel asks, "But have you heard?" (192). When Rachel goes to Calla in desperation, Calla gives her the best gift a friend can give: she promises, "I'll listen" (175).

Finally, Rachel learns to listen to Nick; she listens to him because she loves his voice: "Nick, do you know what I love about you? I love the way your voice sounds, deep but with that scepticism I used to fear and don't fear now" (115). Through listening, she learns to speak: "He's easy to listen to. Easy as well, it almost seems, to reply to. If only it could be that way" (70). "I don't speak openly to him. But I could. I might" (85). She talks to him in her mind, prefacing her thoughts with, "*Listen, Nick* — ": "I talk to him, when he is not here, and tell him everything I can think of, everything that has ever happened, and how I feel" (138). She even begins to echo his voice in his tell-tale phrase, "You know?": "I catch in my own voice something of Nick's — *You know?* I didn't mean to copy. But something of him inhabits me yet" (195).

Finally she learns to speak in fact as well as in fiction. On their first date, she speaks the truth for the very first time, saying, "I hate living here" (68). And on their second date, she is so loquacious that Nick says, "That's the most talking you've done so far, Rachel" (88). Her love affair catapults her into the world of communication. The problems of conception and pregnancy both force her to speak: "I have to speak of it" (103), and "I want to see my sister. Stacey — listen . . . if I could talk to you" (168). She also thinks of Calla, "I wish I could talk to her" (133), and eventually she does confide in Calla. Speaking to Nick, she suggests, "you might teach here," and wonders, "Haven't I any pride?" and answers, "No, I have no pride. None left, not now. This realization renders me all at once calm, inexplicably, and almost free. Have I finished with façades?" (142). This recognition is a breakthrough for Rachel, for finishing with façades gives her freedom, as she emerges from the prison of hypocrisy into the light of liberty. She even learns the liberation of laughter (140), something the clowns downstairs are not capable of.

The turning point in the theme of communication occurs when despair drives Rachel through the valley of the shadow of death, and she confronts her father's phantom, descending the stairs to the underworld where she knocks on the dungeon door. She thinks, "*Let me come in,*" and then says, "Let me come in." Astonished, she wonders, "That was my voice? That pridelessness? It doesn't matter. Suddenly it doesn't matter at all to me" (119). For the first time in the novel, Rachel's inner voice, printed in italics, is echoed by her outer voice, signifying a unification of her split personality, as she steps out of the shadowy wings of fantasy and onto the stage of her real life.

The end of the scene proves that this metamorphosis is not just a flash in the pan. As she leaves, she apologizes as always: "I'm — look, I'm sorry I came down, Hector. I don't know why — I don't know what I was thinking of — ." She reflects, "Go on, Rachel. Apologize. Go on apologizing for ever, go on until nothing of you is left. Is that what you want the most?" She aborts her apology and expresses gratitude: "No — listen, Hector — what I mean is, thanks" (128).

Learning to communicate also involves recognizing the limitations of communication — both the hazards of speaking and the dangers of misinterpretation. Calla reminded Rachel that Saint Paul cautions: "*There are, it may be, so many kinds of voices in the world, and none of them is without signification. Therefore if I know not the meaning of the voice, I shall be unto him that speaketh a barbarian, and he that speaketh shall be a barbarian unto me*" (135). Rachel acknowledges "the apostle's appallingly accurate sight" (135), as she recognizes "God's irony — that we should for so long believe it is only the few who speak in tongues" (134).

This Tower of Babel difficulty of human communication is one of the jests of God. When Rachel misinterpreted Nick's mocking maxim, "Trample their egos firmly," she reflected, "I don't know why I take people's words at their surface value. Mine can't be taken so" (63). Nick is a particularly difficult person to read because "He doesn't reveal much. He only appears to talk openly. Underneath, everything is guarded." "I can't tell at all what he's thinking. I never can, not with anyone. Always this futile guessing game" (84–85). Later she reflects, "We talked sometimes, and I tried to hear what he was saying, but I'm not certain I did hear. I may have heard only guarded echoes of his voice. He never spoke of his real life" (154). But, then, neither did Rachel.

Learning to communicate also involves learning to lie — to others, not to oneself. When Rachel begins her affair with Nick, she finds it necessary to lie to her mother in order to preserve her personal life.

On the telephone with Rachel, Nick says, "I like that polite voice of yours. I'm glad it's deceptive, though" (100). When her mother inquires about her plans, Rachel thinks, "It isn't that I want to lie to her. But she invites it, even demands it. Whoever said the truth shall make you free never knew this kind of house" (100). But the truth does set Rachel free finally.

Eventually, Rachel learns not only how to speak, but how to sing. In the opening scene, Rachel hears the schoolchildren outside singing a skipping song, *"The wind blows low, the wind blows high,"* and she substitutes her own name, *"Rachel Cameron says she'll die / For the want of the golden city"* (1). Setting out for her golden city at the end of the novel, she sings the Psalm, *"Make me to hear joy and gladness, that the bones which Thou hast broken may rejoice"* (201). Her final utterance is a song of freedom and affirmation of the future.

### Love: *"Demons and Webs"*

Love is an extension of communication and communication a part of love, for love means being able to reach out to others, to identify and empathize. Rachel learns to love through a summer romance and so progresses on the continuum of communication from speech to touch, from speaking to loving.

"Women like me are an anachronism" (117), Rachel declares, for she is that incongruity, a thirty-four-year-old virgin — so thoroughly has she internalized her mother's repressive attitudes towards sex: *"A woman's most precious possession,"* Rachel thinks in "mother's archaic simper voice" (89–90). When Mrs. Cameron gloats, "I thank my lucky stars I never had a moment's worry with either of my daughters," Rachel thinks bitterly, "Had. Past tense" (58). So tightly has she locked herself into the stereotypical spinster role that it is almost impossible for her to break out of this fossilized shell. When she goes to Doctor Raven for a pregnancy test, he outrages her by confirming complacently, "there's no question of one thing, anyway, with a sensible girl like yourself" (178).

Rachel is in desperate need of romance, as her sexual fantasies and her outbursts in school and church all demonstrate. Her romantic relationships so far have been disastrous, to put it mildly. Her first movie date at fifteen was torture, lest the boy buy her a child's ticket (66), and Saturday night dances at the Flamingo Dancehall were a torment, lest the clown Cluny Macpherson dance with her, exposing her to the hilarity of spectators (61). Her last dance was with a travelling salesman in embalming fluid, suggesting what a social fossil she has become (17). Her only serious suitor was Lennox Cates, but she broke off their relationship years ago when it looked like becoming serious, because she could not see herself as the wife of an uneducated farmer (31), so deeply has she internalized her mother's snobbery.

Rachel's emotional repression is not only sexual, for she cannot love anyone until she learns to love herself. Perhaps when the father she loved died — long after he had died emotionally — he took her ability to love with him to the underworld. For Rachel to return to life, her ability to love must be resurrected. Far from loving other people, she sees them only as threats to her security — cardboard props on the stage of her life. She imagines the motives of friendly gestures, like Calla's gifts, to be hostility rather than affection.

The three outbursts in the first three chapters of the novel involve three different kinds of love: first, love of men in the sexual fantasy where she conjures up "the shadow prince"; second, love for children in the schoolroom where she involuntarily strikes James Doherty; and third, love of God in the Tabernacle where Rachel is given the gift of tongues. Although Rachel needs all three kinds of love, she has lost the ability to distinguish between them, for all her outbursts are partly sexual. Her affection for her pupils, her love of God, and her bond with her dead father are all confused with her need for normal sexual love. Perhaps Rachel has never weaned her affections away from her father, the first man in her life; when he died, she froze into a state of arrested adolescence. Significantly, Laurence juxtaposes Rachel's deliberate sexual fantasy with her involuntary nightmare of the kingdom of death. When she summons "the shadow prince," who remains faceless and voiceless, like the "unspeaking ones" downstairs, surely she is summoning him from the underworld. The juxtaposition of the two dreams suggests that the shadow prince may also be the king of the dead, her own father. Before Rachel can learn to love normally, she must lay the phantom of her father to rest.

Although her affection for James Doherty, and all of her pupils, obviously results from frustrated maternal impulses, Rachel's schoolroom outburst also has sexual repercussions. She is attracted to the red-haired ragamuffin, and yearns to touch him. Frustrated because she cannot touch him with tenderness like his mother Grace, Rachel touches him with violence. Suspecting James has drawn "obscene caricatures" (53) of her, she lashes out with her ruler, symbol of her rule, and perhaps phallic symbol as well, causing a thin river of blood, emblem of vitality, to stream down his face to his mouth, prefiguring the river valley where she will come to life by learning to love (52–53).

The outburst in the Tabernacle is also manifestly sexual, though primarily religious. The ocean Rachel imagines the Tabernacle resembling is often taken as a symbol of female nature, as well as the subconscious. Her association of the farmer crouched in prayer beside her with her one serious suitor, Lennox Cates, suggests this connection, and her hysterical outburst comes directly after she hears him moan with passion and observes the blood throbbing in his veins (36). No wonder Calla kisses Rachel, interpreting Rachel's outburst (correctly) as sexual in origin. And surely Rachel's reaction is overdone: "My drawing away is sharp, violent. I feel violated, unclean, as though I would strike her dead if I had the means. . . . My anger feels more than justified, and in some way this is a tremendous relief" (38). Rachel feels threatened by Calla's approach, not because she is potentially homosexual, but because she is starved for physical love. But she worries, "Could a person be Calla's way, without knowing it, only it might be obvious to a man, say, or at least sensed, and then he wouldn't — no that's impossible. It's mad. I must not" (83). So the necessity to prove herself sexually with a male suddenly becomes urgent.

Laurence suggests that all kinds of love — sexual, maternal, and religious — are related, but she also demonstrates that they must not be confused. Rachel has to learn to distinguish between love of God, need for children, and desire for men. Before she can come back to life, she must resurrect her love by laying her father's phantom to rest. The catalyst in her sexual rebirth is Nick Kazlik. Appropriately, "[t]he milkman's son" awakens "[t]he undertaker's daughter" (67), a modern-day sleeping beauty, and brings her back to life by teaching her to love on the fertile green banks of the Wachakwa River Valley.

Nick's first kiss unleashes her sexual desire for the first time: "oh my God. Now I really do want him" (72). Even though she pushes him away when he touches her, she has acknowledged a desire for someone else besides herself and her own onanistic fantasies. Although their first lovemaking in a field under the full moon is not entirely satisfactory — since "It's never much good the first time" (92) — nevertheless, Rachel experiences the sense of peace that Calla said was vouchsafed to those given the gift of tongues: "I don't care about anything, except this peace, this pride, holding him" (91). She thinks, "I'm fantastically happy" (94), and later claims triumphantly, "I have changed" (103). Rachel reaches a turning point in her development when she acknowledges, "Nick — listen — I love you" (114).

The third and last time they make love on the "green edge of a brown river" (143), it is utterly satisfying for both of them. Rachel progresses along the communication continuum from speech to touch, quoting John Donne's line, *"For God's sake hold your tongue and let me love"* (145). She is eager for physical contact, commanding Nick to "take off your clothes" (147) which "mysteriously protect us against one another" (148), and commanding him to "Go into me. Now. Right now" (147). For the first time, she lets herself go, losing consciousness of herself in her awareness of another being: "He inhabits whatever core of me there is. I can move outward to him, knowing he wants what I am, and I can receive him, whatever he is, whatever. And then this tender cruelty, always known to him but never before to me, the unmattering of what either of us is — only important that what we are doing should go on and go on and go on — " (147). For the first time, Rachel experiences a sexual orgasm in the name of Nick: "Nick — *Nick* — Only his name. Only at this moment, his name. The only word" (148). Finally, the word is made flesh. The voice of her body utters for the first time, and this sexual rebirth is like "the beginning of the world" (144) for Rachel, as "The world spinningly returns" (92).

Now that she has learned to love Nick, Rachel can love herself. Learning that another being can "inhabit" (104) the temple of her body, and that she could even give houseroom in her "bonehouse" (182) to an embryo, Rachel learns to live in her own body at last, no longer wearing her own hands "like empty gloves" (8). Even after Nick disappears and her foetus proves ephemeral, "something of him inhabits me yet" (195), leading her to love herself, no longer alienated from her own being.

Once Rachel has learned to love herself through loving Nick, she is able to love others, including Calla, Willard, Hector, and even her own mother. Making love with Nick has made Rachel realize that other people are real, not just pasteboard props on the stage of her own life. As Rachel says to Nick, it is a revelation "Just to feel you living there under your skin" (147). Similarly, she recognizes that other people have feelings and that they may care for her.

Willard Siddley, for example, always intimidated the paranoid Rachel. Behind his dark-rimmed glasses, "His eyes are pallid, like the blue dead eyes of the frozen whitefish we used to get in the winter when I was a child, and I always choked on that fish, recalling the eyes" (7). But when she sees Willard without his glasses, she notes "a look of such vulnerability that I feel almost affectionate towards him" (43). After her summer romance with Nick, Rachel realizes that there is nothing sinister behind Willard's glasses: "Behind his navy-framed glasses there is nothing, nothing lurking, nothing gathering itself to pounce. Only his whitefish eyes, hoping for some slight friendliness from me, possibly, while I sit here conjuring up dragons to scare myself with" (157). Having learned to love, she is able to see Willard from his own point of view: "Suddenly I wonder if what he is asking for, really, is condolence, and if he's asked for it before, and if at times he's asked for various other things I never suspected, admiration or reassurance or whatever it was he didn't own in sufficient quantity. I don't know if he is speaking differently or if I am hearing him differently" (157). Rachel finally realizes that Willard's visits were probably the result not of sadism, but of admiration: "He might, quite simply, think I am attractive, and want, in a mild way, some exchange" (157). Life may be simpler than Rachel ever realized.

Similarly, "Hector's eyes are lynx eyes, cat's eyes, the green slanted cat's eyes of glass marbles" (124), echoing the sinister cat's eyes of her dream vision (59). But when Hector shares his vulnerable point with Rachel, "I look into his face then, and for an instant see him living there behind his eyes" (128).

When she thought of Calla earlier, Rachel reflected, "I ought to feel — what? Pity? No. Liberal-minded people feel compassion — it's nicer. But all I feel is nothing" (76). But later, when she says goodbye to Calla, Rachel realizes, "the truth is that she loves me" (198). When Calla, referring to Rachel's false pregnancy, says, "I'm sorry that things weren't different for you" (197), Rachel acknowledges Calla's love and is generous enough to say, "I'm sorry things weren't different for you. I mean, that I wasn't different" (198).

Gradually, Rachel comes to realize that even her own mother is a human being, not a witch: "She's wondering — *what will become of me?"* (114). Rachel recognizes that Nick "had his own demons and webs" (189), and when she overhears her mother mutter in her sleep, *"Niall always thinks I am so stupid"* (186), she realizes that her mother has had her own private torments. Rachel also acknowledges that "she cares about me" — in other words, her mother-hen fussing is a result of natural maternal affection and not tyrannical power-mongering.

Finally, Rachel develops enough self-confidence to sympathize with her own foolish human nature and enough empathy to pity the Joker himself: "God's mercy on reluctant jesters. God's grace on fools. God's pity on God" (202).

### Identity: Mother of the Woman

Once she has learned to acknowledge the reality of other people, Rachel can develop a sense of her own separate identity. All of Laurence's heroines strive to discover their individual identity. To discover who they are as individuals, however, they must first understand and accept their heritage. So the theme of identity involves a conflict between the individual and community, independence and responsibility, freedom and duty. Laurence never advocates neglecting one's responsibility to one's community, but she believes that we must help ourselves before we can help others, love ourselves before we can love anyone else.

The problem of ancestry is quite simple in *A Jest of God*, for Rachel's only antecedents are her parents. Since her father is dead, emancipation from his domination really means coming to terms with death in order to live, as we saw in the discussion of the theme of death. Since her mother is alive, however, liberating herself from her domination involves learning to be independent.

Laurence comments on Rachel's conflict between individuality and ancestry:

> She tries to break the handcuffs of her own past, but she is self-perceptive enough to recognize that for her no freedom from the shackledom of the ancestors can be total. Her emergence from the tomb-like atmosphere of her extended childhood is a partial defeat — or, looked at in another way, a partial victory.

She is no longer so much afraid of herself as she was. She is beginning to learn the rules of survival. ("Ten" 21)

Rachel is named for the biblical figure "mourning for her children" (181). The name is accurate, for Rachel longs for children, as we can see from her attachment to her pupils, whom she refers to as "my children" (2). But Rachel is not ready to have children, for she herself is still an infant, as Calla's constant epithet "child" emphasizes.

Ever since Rachel returned home to Manawaka fourteen years ago, she has been trapped in a time warp, cocooned in delayed adolescence. Her mother talks to her "as though I were about twelve" (57), and Willard makes her feel like a schoolgirl. Rachel's "old-fashioned" room is exactly the same as it was in her childhood, with a white metal bow decorating the head of her bed "like a starched forgotten hair-ribbon" (16). When she hides her mother's contraceptive device in her cupboard, a straw hat trimmed with pink icing sugar ribbon tumbles out, forming an ironic commentary on Rachel's would-be adult behaviour. Rachel reflects, "What a strangely pendulum life I have, fluctuating in age between extremes, hardly knowing myself whether I am too young or too old" (57).

When we first meet Rachel, she is looking out the schoolroom window at the same schoolyard where she sang the same skipping songs at the same age as her pupils twenty-seven years ago. Rachel is hardly any older than the children she teaches. The reason she feels threatened by her former students grown into alien adolescents is because they represent a stage of development that she has never been able to attain. Priestesses in a mysterious cult, they possess the knowledge that Rachel cannot acquire. Prepubescent still at thirty-four years of age, Rachel has never matured into adulthood.

Perhaps that is why her lover Nick Kazlik provides the catalyst for Rachel's development, since her virginity has become a trap, imprisoning her in infancy. We have seen in the discussion of love how her summer romance with Nick inspires her to defy her mother's unreasonable domination: "This newfound ruthlessness exhilarates me. I won't turn back. If I do, I'm done for" (101), Rachel reflects.

Believing that she is pregnant forces Rachel to grow up even more, for one cannot be a mother if one is still a child. The conflicts she has to cope with and the decisions she has to make force her to mature. "It cost me something, that decision, you know?" (181). Since she has the responsibility for the life of another being, she must take responsibility for her own life. Realizing, "I'm on my own. I never knew before what that would be like. It means no one. Just that. Just — myself" (165), Rachel finally becomes an independent adult.

The shock of learning that Nick is married (as he deceives her into thinking) blasts Rachel out of her daydream into the harsh light of reality: "The layers of dream are so many, so many false membranes grown around the mind, that I don't even know they are there until some knifing reality cuts through, and I see the sight of my other eyes for what it has been, distorted, bizarre, grotesque, unbearably a joke if viewed from the outside" (150–51). While everyone dreams, maturity means being able to distinguish inner from outer reality.

The jest of God embodied in the benign tumour completes Rachel's growth, for she has now become wise enough to accept her human foolishness: "All that. And this at the end of it. I was always afraid that I might become a fool. Yet I could almost smile with some grotesque lightheadedness at that fool of a fear, that poor fear of fools, now that I really am one" (181).

Rachel has not delivered a child, but she has given birth to an adult self. Moreover, she has become a mother — of her own "elderly child" (201), for Rachel realizes, *I am the mother now"* (184). Gradually, as Rachel has matured, her symbiotic relationship with her repressive mother has reversed: now that Rachel has become an adult, her aging mother has reverted to childishness. Earlier, Rachel committed an unconscious slip, thinking, "Surely I love her as much as most parents love their children. I mean, of course, as much as most children love their parents" (114). The Freudian slip is prophetic, for Rachel does become the parent figure, as all children do eventually.

Thus, identity and community, individuality and responsibility are really compatible after all. Through developing confidence and self-reliance, Rachel learns to see her mother as a vulnerable human being, not a power-hungry gorgon. Maybe her misinterpretation of her mother's concern was merely the result of her own paranoia. Rachel realizes, "She cares about me" (94), and she is afraid of *"what will become of me"* (114). Hearing her mother murmur in her sleep, *"Niall always thinks I am so stupid"* (186), Rachel realizes that her mother is vulnerable too. Finally, she plays the parental role, reassuring her mother, *"Hush, it will be all right — there, there.* I am the mother now" (196).

Recognizing the reality of her mother's weak heart, Rachel also realizes that she is not responsible for keeping her mother alive: "I really wonder now why I have been so ruthlessly careful of her, as though to preserve her throughout eternity, a dried flower under glass. It isn't up to me. It never was. I can take care, but only some. I'm not responsible for keeping her alive. There is, suddenly, some enormous relief in this realization" (195). Rachel realizes that only God has the power of life and death: when her mother asks who knows what is best for her if Doctor Raven does not, Rachel replies (only partly in jest), "God, for all I know" (195). "My mother's tricky heart will just have to take its own chances" (176), she decides.

Embarking on her adult life at last, Rachel anticipates the possibility of marrying and having children, but her optimism is tempered now with realism:

> Where I'm going, anything may happen. Nothing may happen. Maybe I will marry a middle-aged widower, or a longshoreman, or a cattle-hoof-trimmer, or a barrister or a thief. And have my children in time. Or maybe not. Most of the chances are against it. But not, I think, quite all. What will happen? What will happen. It may be that my children will always be temporary, never to be held. But so are everyone's. (201)

Rachel's final affirmation of life reflects her creator's philosophy: Margaret Laurence wrote, "Optimism in this world seems impossible to me. But in each novel there is some hope, and that is a different thing entirely" (*Heart* 6).

## ALLUSIONS: MULTIPLE VOICES

Margaret Laurence is a very literary novelist, a well-read writer who is inspired by her literary ancestors. All of her novels include many explicit quotations from and implicit allusions to famous works of literature. She quotes frequently from the Bible, the most influential book in our literary heritage, but she also quotes many other writers from the English literary tradition. The biblical and literary quotations in *A Jest of God* are distinguished by italic print, like Rachel's silent thoughts. A truly polyphonic author, perhaps Laurence is trying to find her individual voice amid the myriad eloquent voices of our cultural heritage, just as Rachel is trying to find her own voice among the multiple voices she inherits from her ancestors.

## Biblical Allusions

### Rachel

Laurence makes rich use of biblical allusions that extend the significance of her characters' situations to embrace the history of humankind. And her characters often learn, consciously or unconsciously, from their biblical models or namesakes. Rachel Cameron's Christian name inevitably connects her with the biblical Rachel. The voice of Rachel is "mourning for her children" (181), like her biblical namesake: "Thus saith the LORD; A voice was heard in Ramah, lamentation, *and* bitter weeping; Rachel weeping for her children refused to be comforted for her children, because they *were* not" (Jeremiah 31.15).

Rachel Cameron is named for the Genesis Rachel. The Genesis story recounts how Jacob came to visit his uncle Laban and fell in love with Laban's younger daughter Rachel while she was watering her father's flocks at the well: "And it came to pass, when Jacob saw Rachel the daughter of Laban his mother's brother, and the sheep of Laban his mother's brother, that Jacob went near, and rolled the stone from the well's mouth, and watered the flock of Laban his mother's brother. And Jacob kissed Rachel, and lifted up his voice, and wept" (Genesis 29.10–11).

Jacob labours for seven years for Laban to win Rachel in marriage, but on their wedding night Laban substitutes the elder daughter Leah because the younger daughter is not supposed to be married before the elder. Laban then demands that Jacob labour yet another seven years for Rachel, totalling fourteen years in all. When Jacob and Rachel are finally married, however, Rachel proves barren, unlike her elder more fruitful sister Leah: "And when the LORD saw that Leah *was* hated, he opened her womb: but Rachel *was* barren" (29.31).

Similarly, Rachel Cameron has an elder and more fruitful sister named Stacey, who has escaped the manacles of Manawaka to live in Vancouver with her husband Clifford MacAindra and their four children. Stacey's story is recounted in Laurence's subsequent novel

*The Fire-Dwellers* (1969). Rachel is jealous of her sister Stacey and wishes she had children too: "And when Rachel saw that she bare Jacob no children, Rachel envied her sister" (30.1).

Like her biblical namesake, Rachel Cameron longs for children, but, as an unmarried woman, she has been denied them. Instead, she views her pupils as her children, although she knows she must not. When she finally has a love affair with Nick Kazlik, one of her motives is the desire for children: frustrated maternal instinct finally leads her to hint to Nick, "If I had a child, I would like it to be yours" (148). She screams silently, *"Give me my children"* (148), echoing her biblical namesake's cry to Jacob, "Give me children, or else I die" (30.1). Unlike God, however, Nick cannot make this Rachel fruitful; recognizing his impotence, he cautions, "I'm not God. I can't solve anything" (148).

Laurence underlines the biblical parallel by calling Calla's canary Jacob, the name of the biblical figure who married Rachel. Jacob also wrestled with the angel and had a vision of angels climbing a ladder to heaven in Genesis (32.24). Calla whistles, *"She's Only a Bird in a Gilded Cage"* (47), suggesting that Jacob is a humorous symbol for Rachel, who is also imprisoned in a metaphorical cage. Calla names her canary Jacob because "All he does is march up and down that blasted ladder. . . . Maybe the angel at the top can't be seen by me" (137). Like Jacob, Rachel has not yet found her voice; the question will be, can she see the angel at the top of her ladder.

## Jonah

Another important biblical allusion in *A Jest of God* is to the story of Jonah and the whale. Laurence first refers to Jonah in the epigraph to the novel drawn from Carl Sandburg's poem "Losers," from his book *Smoke and Steel* (1920):

> *If I should pass the tomb of Jonah*
> *I would stop there and sit for awhile;*
> *Because I was swallowed one time deep in the dark*
> *And came out alive after all.*

Jonah is another biblical parallel for Rachel: like Jonah, Rachel has been swallowed deep in the dark, and, like Jonah, she comes out alive after all. Hector Jonas, the undertaker who helps Rachel emerge from her tomb, reinforces the biblical parallel by echoing the name of Jonah in his own patronymic.

The book of Jonah tells the story of how God commissioned Jonah to take the word of God to the wicked city of Nineveh, but Jonah fled from God's mission and took ship to Tarshish to escape the Lord. God sent a tempest that threatened to sink the ship: "the LORD sent out a great wind into the sea, and there was a mighty tempest in the sea, so that the ship was like to be broken" (Jonah 1.4). Knowing that he was the cause, Jonah advised the sailors to throw him overboard: "And he said unto them, Take me up, and cast me forth into the sea; so shall the sea be calm unto you: for I know that for my sake this great tempest *is* upon you" (1.12). Jonah's prediction is fulfilled: "So they took up Jonah, and cast him forth into the sea: and the sea ceased from her raging" (1.15).

But Jonah's problems have only begun: "Now the LORD had prepared a great fish to swallow up Jonah. And Jonah was in the belly of the fish three days and three nights" (1.17). After this purgatorial suffering, Jonah prays to God for deliverance: "Then Jonah prayed unto the LORD his God out of the fish's belly, And said, I cried by reason of mine affliction unto the LORD, and he heard me; out of the belly of hell cried I, *and* thou heardest my voice" (2.1–2). But God forgives Jonah's disobedience: "And the LORD spake unto the fish, and it vomited out Jonah upon the dry *land*" (2.10). Delivered, Jonah carries out God's mission and journeys to Nineveh to preach the word of God to that wicked city.

Rachel is a modern Jonah. Resurrection from what Laurence terms "the tomb-like atmosphere of her extended childhood" ("Ten" 21) is essential for Rachel. The winds of tempest that God sent to engulf Jonah are also overwhelming Rachel. Stretched out in her bathtub, with its "claw feet taloned and grasping like a griffin's," Rachel considers that her "flesh does have a drowned look," as she recalls Shakespeare's *Tempest* and Melville's *Moby Dick*, a novel about a whale (137–39). Like Jonah, who cried, "The waters compassed me about, *even* to the soul" (2.5), Rachel also fears she has "drowned" in the depths of her depression.

Like Jonah, Rachel also falls on her knees and prays to God, the "last resort": *"Help me."* But, unlike Jonah, Rachel does not hear any reply: "If You have spoken, I am not aware of having heard. If You have a voice, it is not comprehensible to me. No omens. No burning bush, no pillar of sand by day or pillar of flame by night" (171) — alluding to the voice of God that spoke to Moses out of the bush which burned but was not consumed. Even though Rachel does not hear the voice of God, she is delivered: after her prayer to God, which forms the turning point of the novel, Rachel finds within herself the strength to endure.

## Saint Paul

Laurence also quotes directly from Saint Paul's first Epistle to the Corinthians in two significant places. First, in the scene at the Tabernacle, the preacher quotes Saint Paul on the gifts of the Spirit to emphasize the themes of self-knowledge and self-expression: *"Now there are diversities of gifts, but the same Spirit. For to one is given by the Spirit the word of wisdom — to another the word of knowledge — to another the gifts of healing — to another prophecy — to another divers kinds of tongues — "* (33). Calla Mackie quotes the words of Saint Paul that underline Laurence's theme of voices: *"I thank my God I speak with tongues more than ye all"* (27). Later she quotes Saint Paul cautioning against speaking in tongues: *"There are, it may be, so many kinds of voices in the world, and none of them is without signification. Therefore if I know not the meaning of the voice, I shall be unto him that speaketh a barbarian, and he that speaketh shall be a barbarian unto me"* (135). Speech should be communication. Calla continues to quote Paul's first Epistle to the Corinthians — *"God is not the author of confusion but of peace, as in all the churches of the saints"* (33) — emphasizing that the gift of tongues brings peace, not the babbling confusion of the Tower of Babel. Later, Calla quotes Saint Paul saying, *"If any man among you thinketh himself to be wise, let him become a fool, that he may be wise"* (135). The next verse declares, "For the wisdom of this world is foolishness with God" (1 Corinthians 3.19). Psalm 53 begins, "The fool hath said in his heart, *There is* no God" (1). This is the lesson of faith and foolishness that Rachel must learn.

## Miscellaneous Biblical Allusions

Rachel also quotes The Song of Solomon (2.7) ironically when she reminds herself that "Women shouldn't phone men": *"I adjure you,*

*O daughters of Jerusalem, by the roes and by the hinds of the field, that ye stir not up, nor awaken love, until it please"* (131–32). Nick also quotes the prophet Jeremiah significantly: *"I have forsaken my house — I have left mine heritage — mine heritage is unto me as a lion in the forest — it crieth out against me — therefore have I hated it"* (110). This allusion explains Nick's ambivalent attitude towards his own heritage — the dairy farm that his milkman father Nestor the Jester wants him to inherit in place of his dead twin Steve. Rachel parallels Nick, for she too is torn between her responsibility to her parents and her responsibility to herself.

Rachel also quotes the Gospel ironically: "Seek and ye shall find" (32). But the quotation proves a prophecy, for Rachel finally does find faith. At the end of her narrative, she quotes Psalm 51, verse 8: *"Make me to hear joy and gladness, that the bones which Thou hast broken may rejoice"* (201). Like Job, Rachel has suffered, and, like Job, she has finally learned joy.

### Literary Allusions

Laurence also uses allusions to other literary works to underline her themes. The epigraph to the novel, as we have seen, is drawn from Carl Sandburg's poem "Losers" and introduces the parable of Jonah and the whale. But Sandburg's losers win, as we shall see. We also saw how Rachel's reference to Shakespeare's *Tempest* reinforces the concept of drowning in a storm at sea involved in the biblical story of Jonah and the whale, while her reference to *Moby Dick*, Herman Melville's novel about Captain Ahab's war of wills with a whale, underlines the parallels with Jonah's ordeal in the whale's belly.

Laurence alludes to ancient Greek as well as to modern English literature. For example, Hector Jonas and Nestor Kazlik are both named for classical figures from ancient Greek literature: Hector is the name of King Priam's son killed by Achilles in Homer's *Iliad*, and Nestor is the name of Odysseus's father in Homer's *Odyssey*. In the Tabernacle scene, Rachel terms the speaker in tongues "a younger Tiresias come to tell the king the words that no one could listen to and live" (35) — the blind seer who told King Oedipus that he had murdered his father and married his mother in Sophocles' play *Oedipus Rex*. The congregation reminds Rachel of the Bacchae, worshippers of Dionysus, a Greek god associated with drunkenness and erotic love (36). Eventually Rachel thinks she has become "Mad as any Grecian woman on the demented and blood-lit hills" (116).

Rachel views other people as a kind of Greek chorus commenting on the tragedy of her blighted life, "an unseen audience ready to hoot and caw with a shocking derision" (95) — chanting "like a Greek chorus . . . *Dead, dead, dead*" (107). Ultimately, however, Rachel and Hector impersonate Persephone and Pluto figures, as Rachel leaves the underworld of Hades and returns to the living earth.

Rachel recalls walking alone on the hill beyond the cemetery to look for crocuses in the early spring and remembering the lines from William Wordsworth's poem "Daffodils": *"I wandered lonely as a cloud* — like some anachronistic survival of Romantic pantheism, collecting wildflowers, probably, to press between the pages of the *Encyclopaedia Britannica"* (80). When her love affair involves her in deception, she recalls the famous lines from Sir Walter Scott's "Marmion":

*Oh what a tangled web we weave*
*When first we practise to deceive!* (77)

Nick reassures Rachel that the field where he wants to make love is "as private as the grave," recalling to her mind these lines from Andrew Marvell's seduction poem "To His Coy Mistress" that express the *carpe diem* theme of "Gather ye roses while ye may" to underline the importance of living and loving while you can:

*The grave's a fine and private place*
*But none, I think, do there embrace.* (90)

Afterwards, Rachel laments, *"My reputation — I've lost my reputation.* Who said that? Some nitwit in Shakespeare" (92) — Cassio in *Othello*, in fact. When next they make love, Rachel is so eager that she tacitly speaks the opening line from John Donne's poem "The Canonization": *"For God's sake hold your tongue and let me love"* (145). And when Rachel considers abortion, she paraphrases lines from Rudyard Kipling's "Harp Song of the Dane Women" from *Puck of Pooks Hill*:

*What is woman that you forsake her*
*To the claws of the grey old angel-maker?* (116)

Rachel has a literary quotation for every crisis.

Laurence also sings others' songs, both nursery rhymes and hymns. Rachel dreams that "My mother is singing in a falsetto voice, the stylish tremolo, the ladies' choir voice. *Bless this house dear Lord we pray, keep it safe by night and day*" (19) — ironic, since theirs is a house of death. The Presbyterian Church that the Camerons patronize is contrasted with the non-conformist Tabernacle of the Risen and Reborn through its hymns. The Presbyterian church sings decorous hymns, like *"The Church's One Foundation"* (40) and *"Jerusalem the Golden"* (42), whereas the Tabernacle sings hymns full of violent passion:

> *Day of wrath! O day of mourning!*
> *See fulfilled the prophet's warning!*
> *Heaven and earth in ashes burning!* (32)

This hymn suggests the end of the world wreaked in revenge by the Old Testament God of Vengeance. The next hymn they sing suggests an erotic embrace:

> *In full and glad surrender,*
> *I give myself to Thee,*
> *Thine utterly and only*
> *And evermore to be.* (34)

The last hymn expresses the joy conspicuously absent from the sober tones of the Presbyterian service:

> *Rejoice! Rejoice! Emmanuel*
> *Shall come to thee, O Israel!* (35)

But the hymn sung at the Presbyterian church is actually an important one for Rachel. Although Laurence only quotes four lines, it is worth quoting the first verse in full, for this hymn relates to Rachel's vision of a "golden city" voiced in the opening nursery rhyme:

> *Jerusalem the golden,*
> *With milk and honey blest —*
> *Beneath thy contemplation*
> *Sink heart and voice oppressed*
> *I know not, oh, I know not*

*What social joys are there*
*What radiancy of glory*
*What light beyond compare.*

Hector Jonas plays two hymns for Rachel on his organ in the mortuary: first Bach's chorale *"Jesu Joy of Man's Desiring"* for "[t]he carriage trade" (126) and then this saccharine song that reflects Rachel's golden vision:

*There is a happy land*
*Far far away — ...*
*Where saints and angels stand*
*Bright, bright as day —* (127)

The vision of a golden world reflected in these last two hymns relates to the nursery rhyme that opens Rachel's narrative, introducing her ideal goal:

*The wind blows low, the wind blows high*
*The snow comes falling from the sky,*
*Rachel Cameron says she'll die*
*For the want of the golden city.*
  *She is handsome, she is pretty,*
  *She is the queen of the golden city —* (1)

Rachel desires her city of gold, but fears the winds of change that might waft her thither. She recites to herself two other sinister skipping songs that reflect some of her paranoia:

*Spanish dancers, turn around,*
*Spanish dancers, get out of this town.* (1)

This rhyme suggests Rachel's own sense of alienation and exclusion. The next one may suggest her father's rejection of her mother in favour of his corpses:

*Nebuchadnezzar, King of the Jews,*
*Sold his wife for a pair of shoes.* (2)

Later, Calla Mackie whistles, *"She's Only a Bird in a Gilded Cage"* (47), suggesting that Rachel is trapped in a cage of her own creation. Eventually, Rachel will liberate herself sufficiently to sing a song of joy: *"Make me to hear joy and gladness, that the bones which Thou has broken may rejoice*" (201). So in giving her characters "the gift of tongues," Laurence teaches her heroines not only how to speak but how to sing.

## IMAGERY: THE DEEP THEATRE OF THE MIND

Margaret Laurence uses imagery to reveal themes in all of her novels, especially *A Jest of God*. Rachel Cameron is a very imaginative woman, like her creator, and her perceptions of internal and external reality are very vivid. Since she is the narrator of the novel, her imaginative perception dominates the narrative. Her paranoid impressions are particularly vivid: "The darkening sky is hugely blue, gashed with rose, blood, flame pouring from the volcano or wound or flower of the lowering sun. The wavering green, the sea of grass, piercingly bright. Black tree trunks, contorted, arching over the river" (85). Rachel's distorted perception of external reality is colourful and artistic — like Van Gogh's impressionistic paintings of starlight skies and chrysanthemums in his late paranoid period. Rachel's internal scenery is equally paranoid: "When I close my eyes, I see scratches of gold against the black, and they form into jagged lines, teeth, a knife's edge, the sharp hard hackles of dinosaurs" (58–59).

Rachel's imaginary world, the "deep theatre" (90) of the mind, where "I dramatize myself" (4), is terrifying too, because Rachel imagines "an unseen audience ready to hoot and caw with a shocking derision" (95). She views the Cameron Funeral Home as "the stage-set of a drama that never was enacted" (124). Rachel perceives people as clowns, masked with make-up, like the people "painted and prettified" (2) for burial, and she feels "like a papier mâché doll jerked by a drunken puppetmaster" (82). Her dream of death introduces many of the major motifs of the novel, as her masturbation fantasy of a "shadow prince" gives way to an involuntary nightmare of the kingdom of death, peopled by clowns:

> Stairs rising from nowhere, and the wallpaper the loose-petalled unknown flowers. The stairs descending to the place where I am not allowed. The giant bottles and jars stand there, bubbled green glass. The silent people are there, lipsticked and rouged,

powdered whitely like clowns. How funny they look, each lying dressed in best, and their open eyes are glass eyes, cat's eye marbles, round glass beads, blue and milky, unwinking. (19)

Rachel is obsessed with eyes watching her: running the gauntlet of eyes, she imagines that "the eyes all around have swollen to giants' eyes" (48), and that everyone is staring at her — even the "golden cats with seeing eyes" (59) of her erotic fantasies and the corpses with their "glass eyes, cat's eye marbles, round glass beads, blue and milky, unwinking" (19) of her nightmares. The eyes of the living are also "opaque, not to be seen through" (52). Willard Siddley's eyes are "pallid, like the blue dead eyes of the frozen whitefish" (7), although his eyes appear vulnerable when divested of his thick, dark-rimmed glasses (43). "Hector's eyes are lynx eyes, cat's eyes, the green slanted cat's eyes of glass marbles" (124), but later, Rachel sees him "living there behind his eyes" (128).

Rachel, the untouchable, is also obsessed by hands because she wears her own hands "like empty gloves" (8). Both fascinated and repelled by "Willard Siddley's spotted furry hands" (9), she feels compelled to touch them because "[w]ith them he touches his wife, and holds the strap to strike a child, and — " (44). Eventually she will learn to use her hands for loving, not hurting.

Rachel is even afraid to see her own reflection in the mirror: "I can't succeed in avoiding my eyes in the mirror. The narrow angular face stares at me, the grey eyes too wide for it" (16). The mirror symbolizes her split personality, reflecting her shadowy twin: "I can see myself in the mirror, not quite but almost, the silver fishwhite of arms, the crane of a body, gaunt metal or gaunt bird" (115). Store windows, like the distorting mirrors of a funhouse, reflect Rachel's zombie self: "I can see myself reflected dimly, like the negative of a photography . . . a thin streak of a person, like the stroke of a white chalk on a chalkboard" (29). Windows can act like magic mirrors, especially in the opening scene, where Rachel observes through the schoolroom window her phantom childhood self reincarnated in her pupils. When she enters the mirror like Alice through the looking-glass, she panics: "In the long wall mirror I saw myself running, the white of my dress, the featureless face, the tallness, a thin stiff white feather like a goose's feather, caught up and hurtled along by some wind no one else could feel" (153).

Rachel sees herself as a skeleton, symbol of death. She is obsessed with "[t]he skull beneath the skin" (122), sign of death, and the throbbing inside her own skull (18), sign of life. One suitor, a travelling salesman in embalming fluid, admired her for her "good bones" (17). Rachel regards gravely her own "cross of bones" in the bath, like a corpse laid out for burial (139).

Rachel's self-image also reveals her inferiority complex. In her imagination, the "deep theatre of the mind," she is beautiful, as we can see in the opening nursery rhyme: *"She is handsome, she is pretty, / She is the queen of the golden city"* (1). But in reality, she thinks she is too tall and skinny, like a scrawny sapling: "My arms . . . seem so long and skinny" (3), and "My own hands, spread out on the desk, are too large. Large and too thin, like empty gloves" (8).

Rachel feels threatened by the teenage girls with their masks of make-up, jewelled eyes and lacquered hair — like the painted clowns in the mortuary. Her own hair is done in "nondescript waves, mole brown" (12), as always. She feels her clothes are not stylish or becoming: her unfashionably long dress "seems like sackcloth, flapping around my knees. And the ashes, where are they?" (4). When she tries to look stylish in the white hooded raincoat, her image reflected in a store window reveals that she resembles a spectre in an ancient robe (29). She looks like a walking zombie and feels "like a clay figurine, easily broken, unmendable" (46), or "like a papier mâché doll jerked by a drunken puppetmaster" (82). Her enigmatic smile suggests to Willard Siddley the Sphinx or the Mona Lisa (6).

Rachel compares herself to animals: "In the hall mirror I can see this giraffe woman, this lank scamperer" (75) or "a Saint Bernard galloping to the rescue of some stranded Alpine party" (140), as she charges for the telephone. Her acquaintances are also characterized as animals, representing the threat they appear to the paranoid Rachel: Nestor the Jester Kazlik is "a great bear of a man" (69), Teresa Kazlik is "like some kind of stout silent tortoise" (70), and Cluny Macpherson is "like a bulldog" (61). Willard seems "reptilian" (45), like a lizard (8), and the solitary Chinese man, Lee Toy, is symbolized by his wall painting of "a solitary and splendidly plumaged tiger" (50). Calla Mackie's fringe of hair reminds Rachel of a Shetland pony (3), her mother going to church in her new flowered-silk coat walks "like a butterfly released from winter" (40), and Nick slithers out of his flannels "like a snake shrugging off its last year's skin" (90) —

like the snake he turns out to be. The congregation of the Tabernacle reminds her of the sinister beast-men in H.G. Wells's *The Island of Dr. Moreau* (31), and she fears that Calla will "wail in a wolf's voice, or speak as hissingly as a cell of serpents" (31). Even the bathtub seems like a fabled beast, "mounted on claw feet taloned and grasping like a griffin's" (137), and her pupils "troop in, two by two, all the young animals into my Ark" (154).

Rachel also characterizes her acquaintances as birds — often birds of prey that threaten her: Willard looks like a vulture bending over her desk (23), Tom Gillanders looks like "an emaciated crow" in "his black choir gown" (42), and Calla looks like "a great horned owl" in her heavy-rimmed glasses (26). James takes off like a sparrow when he leaves her class (3), and Rachel fears that the other students will fall on her like falcons if she apologizes to James for striking him (53). Doctor Raven is named for the harbinger of death (176), and Hector warns Rachel that she will be "a dead duck" if she lingers in the mortuary (128). Rachel's own self-image is often that of "gaunt birds" (115) — a crane (115) or awkward ostrich (177), or "a tame goose trying to fly" (130), for she has yet to try her wings. Most important, though, is the bird image that Rachel fails to recognize — Calla's silent songbird Jacob, symbolizing the repressed Rachel (47).

The novel is also filled with angels — birds of a different feather — suggesting the Providence that short-sighted Rachel fails to see. The angels that Rachel imagines at first are sinister figures, "the Angel of Death" (94) or the "Angel-makers" (116) of abortionists. Contemplating her mother's antique contraceptive device, Rachel paraphrases Kipling's couplet about the sea: *"What is woman that you forsake her / To the claws of the grey old angel-maker?"* (116). She sees Doctor Raven as "some deputy angel allotted the job of the initial sorting out of sheep and goats" (176). Rachel says bitterly, "Laugh, angels" (116), but eventually she learns to laugh with them. Hector Jonas sings her a song about a bright and happy land *"Where saints and angels stand"* (127), and she recalls "a joke about an angel who traded his harp for an upright organ" (126). The angel that is the star of Rachel's celestial aviary, however, is the invisible one at the top of Jacob's ladder (137), recalling the creatures that adorn James's *"splendid"* spaceship, "like angels climbing Jacob's ladder" (6).

*A Jest of God* is full of cages, symbolizing the psychological prison in which Rachel is trapped. Calla whistles, *"She's Only a Bird in a*

*Gilded Cage,*" suggesting the cage that Rachel has created for herself (47). Her mother is like a deadly Iron Maiden, "circling my wrist with her white sapphire-ringed hand" (101), making her feel "as though a leather thong had lassoed my temples" (81). Even her unnaturally prolonged virginity feels like "an oxen yoke" (92) that she longs to throw off, but her dilemma about contraception makes her feel she is being crushed "between millstones" (94). Manawaka itself is a prison of propriety where she feels "boxed-in" (88), "bounded by trivialities" (82).

But *A Jest of God* boasts stairs and ladders to escape from prison. The Jacob's ladder in Calla's canary's cage and the ladder to heaven on James Doherty's celestial spaceship both suggest Rachel's eventual ascent. The faded flowered stairs down to the mortuary haunt Rachel's dreams (19), however, until she discovers the courage to descend them to confront Death in his own kingdom (118). Liberated at last by Hector Jonas, she can ascend the stairs back to life: "The carpeted stairs have to be climbed one at a time" (128). Hardly a Houdini, Rachel later learns that Hector plans to erect a ladder outside her window, symbolizing her successful escape trick (200).

Settings are symbolic in Laurence's Manawaka novels, and Rachel's existence in the tomb over the funeral parlour where her father reigned as king of the dead emphasizes her living death. In the discussions of Manawaka, we saw how Laurence employs the town of Manawaka as a moralized landscape, symbolizing the themes of the novel. Manawaka itself is divided culturally by the proverbial railway tracks, and even the churches, as we saw, toe that line.

Laurence employs pictures and signs to symbolize the values embodied in the novel's two churches. The contrasting portraits of "Jesus, bearded and bleeding" (30) in the Tabernacle of the Risen and Reborn and the "slightly effeminate insurance salesman" (41) of the Presbyterian Church represent their different religious values. The Tabernacle also boasts a bright crimson sign, as well as a "blue and red glass circle of a rose-window at the very top" (29), to symbolize its vitality. The evolution of the funeral parlour sign from sombre black to flashing red and blue neon lights like a night club and the gradual disappearance of the crucial word "funeral" symbolize Manawaka's refusal to acknowledge the reality of death (13).

The portraits of "The Strawberry Girl" and "simpering puce-mouthed Madonna" (67) symbolize the complacent repressions of

Rachel's home, but the "gilt-bordered ikon, and an embroidered tablecloth with some mythical tree nestled in by a fantasy of birds" (102) in the Kazlik home represent their nurturing ethnic background. The dairy is "as newly white as an egg" (101), symbolizing new life.

Colours are symbolic too, as the egg-white dairy suggests, for the Tabernacle is painted eggshell and moss-green, colours of birth and growth. Mrs. Cameron is symbolized by mauve, the colour her lips turn when she has a heart attack and the colour of her blood — somewhere between red and blue. The courage to use brilliant colours is a sign of vitality. Calla Mackie paints her door purple, whereas Mrs. Cameron tells Rachel her orange scarf is too bright to wear to church (40). Niall Cameron's black undertaker's sign contrasts with Hector Jonas' red and blue ones, and the Tabernacle's crimson sign and red and blue rose window symbolize its vitality. Doctor Raven is colour-coded for death, whereas James Doherty's red hair (and red blood) is sign of life. The fourteen sleeping pills that Rachel takes in her suicide attempt (one for each of her years as a school teacher in Manawaka *and* for Jacob's years of labour for his Rachel) are red and blue also, symbolizing life and death. Rachel employs legacies from both her parents — her mother's sleeping pills and her father's spirits — to kill herself, but impulsively throws them onto the mortuary lawn. Gold symbolizes Rachel's goal, the colour of her *"golden city"* (1) and "Jerusalem the Golden," God's promised land of *"milk and honey"* (42).

The landscape is also significant, as Laurence contrasts town and country: Galloping Mountain, where Nick's uncle lives, and Diamond Lake, where Rachel recalls the crazy loon voices of her childhood, represent pure places still unadulterated by the hypocrisies of the town. Manawaka's only link with that ideal world of nature is the Wachakwa River. Symbol of natural freedom and love, the river valley is the escape route for schoolboys and lovers alike. Rachel will come to life on the banks of the river when Nick awakens her, a modern-day Sleeping Beauty. Strange bedfellows, the river valley lies next to the cemetery (79), symbolizing the unending cycle of life and death.

Laurence makes rich use of seasonal symbolism to represent the development of her protagonist. *A Jest of God* begins in early spring (10), Rachel flowers in the summer romance, and (after Rachel is "deflowered") the love affair fades with the approach of autumn. Floral imagery symbolizes Rachel's evolution.

Rachel asks her pupils if they have found any pussywillows, harbingers of spring (4). She remembers one spring searching by the cemetery for crocuses under the snow — "among the stalks of last year's grass now brittle and brown like the ancient bones of birds, the crocuses were growing, the flowers' faint mauve protected by the green-grey hairs of the outer petals" — and recalls Wordsworth's poem, "I Wandered Lonely as a Cloud" (79). Her friend Calla, named by her mother for the lily that symbolizes death and rebirth at Easter, but who is more like a sunflower — "brash, strong, plain, and yet reaching up in some way" (9) — initiates the central theme of rebirth by bringing Rachel a gift of "a hyacinth, bulbously in bud and just about to give birth to the blue-purple blossom" (9) — prefiguring Rachel's putative pregnancy and her ultimate delivery.

Rachel's home is in the Japonica Funeral Chapel watched over by the "delphinium blinking of eyes" (68) of the blue neon sign on Japonica Street (ironically named for a red flower). The "trampled roses" (118) on the steps down to the mortuary are the primrose path to death. When Rachel escapes from death, she dreams she is "running across thick grass and small purple violets" (19). The rose window on the Tabernacle of the Risen and Reborn symbolizes resurrection, but it is not until Rachel delivers her tumour of death that she is reborn as a real woman. After her surgery, her pupils send her "russet asters" in autumn colours, while Calla sends "a dozen yellow roses" and Willard sends a practical potted begonia (184), symbols of her survival.

Trees are important to Rachel too, especially the spruce trees that surround her house, "like the greenblack feathered strong-boned wings of giant and extinct birds," "darkly sheltering, shutting out prying eyes or the sun in summer" (13). In her first fantasy, she imagines that she is in a forest where "The trees are green walls, high and shielding, boughs of pine and tamarack, branches sweeping to earth, forming a thousand rooms among the fallen leaves. She is in the green-walled room, the boughs opening just enough to let the sun in, the moss hairy and soft on the earth" (18) — a green house where she can be alone with her "shadow prince" protected from prying eyes. When she first makes love with Nick Kazlik in the Wachakwa River Valley, she is protected by a natural screen of "bluffs of poplar with their always-whispering leaves that are touched into sound by even the slightest wind, and choke-cherry bushes with the clusters of berries still hard and green, and matted screens of wild rose bushes with nearly all their petals fallen, only the yellow dying centre remaining" (83). After she escapes from death in her nightmare, Rachel dreams that "The spruce trees bend, bend down, hemming in and protecting" (19).

The Wachakwa is like the River Jordan where Rachel is baptized by love. Water is symbolic throughout the novel, symbolizing female nature, death, and the subconscious mind. Like Jonah, Rachel drowns and finally surfaces, but only after she has suffered her own sea change. Other fluids besides water are symbolic, especially blood. After Rachel strikes her favourite pupil across the face, she is horrified to see "the thin blood river" (52) stream down his face, symbol of vitality. Rachel is surprised to recall that real blood flows in her veins instead of embalming fluid (117). The Kazlik Dairy's milk is a nurturing fluid, and indeed "[t]he milkman's son" does awaken "[t]he undertaker's daughter" (67) on the banks of the Wachakwa.

Water is a traditional symbol of the subconscious mind: as Rachel sinks into sleep, she thinks, "The night is a jet-black lake. A person could sink down and even disappear without a trace" (59). Sleep is a miniature of death, but when Rachel submerges into her subconscious mind, her desires surface in her dreams, and her fears come to life. Rachel's erotic fantasy of Cleopatra's Roman orgy recapitulates many of the motifs and images that we have considered:

They used to have banquets with dozens there. Hundreds. Egyptian girls and Roman soldiers. Oasis melons, dusty grapes brought in the long ships from somewhere. Goblets shaped like cats, cats with listening ears, engraven in gold, not serpents or bulls, not Israel or Greece, only golden cats, cruelly knowledgeable as Egypt. They drank their wine from golden cats with seeing eyes. And when they'd drunk enough, they would copulate as openly as dogs, a sweet hot tangle of the smooth legs around the hard hairy thighs. The noise and sweat — the sound of their breath — the slaves looking on, having to stand itchingly immobile while they watched the warm squirming of those —
(59)

As Rachel develops, she learns to confront her desires and fears in reality and not just in her dreams — as we will see in the discussion of Rachel's development in the section on structures.


## NARRATIVE VOICE

A novel tells a story, and the way that story is told is significant. *A Jest of God* is told in the first person and the present tense, as the central character, Rachel Cameron, tells her own tale. So Rachel is both protagonist and narrator, both heroine and reporter of the drama of her own life. Consequently, her confessional narrative will be real and immediate, straight from the horse's mouth. But it will also be ironic, because Rachel may misinterpret the facts she records. So the reader must be alert to catch the clues Rachel misses.

In her 1972 essay, "Time and the Narrative Voice," Margaret Laurence writes: "The treatment of time and the handling of the narrative voice — these two things are of paramount importance to me in the writing of fiction. . . . Most of the fiction I have written in recent years has been written in the first person, with the main character assuming the narrative voice" (156). So character is crucial in determining narrative method, for "it is the character who chooses which parts of the personal past, the family past and the ancestral past have to be revealed in order for the present to be realized and the future to happen" (160).

Early reviewers and critics of *A Jest of God* criticized Laurence's use of first-person, present-tense narration. Clara Thomas judged that "artistically, as a novel, it slides out of balance. Because every-thing comes through Rachel's consciousness and because her mind is so completely, believably, neurotically obsessed, she cannot really see the world around her or the people in it" (*Margaret Laurence* 51). That, of course, is the point: Laurence shows us a schizophrenic character waking up to reality, as the narrative method recreates this development dramatically. Laurence defends her narrative method thus: "*A Jest of God*, as some critics have pointed out disapprovingly, is a very inturned novel. I recognize the limitations of a novel told in the first person and the present tense, from one viewpoint only, but it couldn't have been done any other way, for Rachel herself is a very inturned person" ("Ten" 21). Laurence elaborates in "Gadgetry or Growing: Form and Voice in the Novel":

> I did not want to write another novel in the first person, or at least I *thought* I didn't want to. I tried again and again to begin the novel in the third person, and it simply would not write itself that way. Everything about those first drafts of the first pages was wrong. They were too stilted; the character of Rachel would not reveal herself. So finally I gave up and stopped struggling. I began to write the novel as I really must have very intensely wanted to write it — in the first person, through Rachel's eyes. I knew that this meant the focus of the book was narrow — but so was Rachel's life. . . .
> I felt that present tense was essential in order to convey a sense of immediacy, of everything happening right that moment, and I felt that this sense of immediacy was necessary in order to get across the quality of Rachel's pain and her determined efforts to survive. (84–85)

More recent critics have applauded Laurence's narrative voice in *A Jest of God*. George Bowering, for example, states, "The form of the novel, first person and present tense, works as Rachel's opening-out does, to get naked" (211).

Laurence's narrative method in *A Jest of God* mirrors Rachel's dilemma perfectly. The heroine is her own narrator: "the thin giant She" (1) is both our "I" and our "eye." Rachel's narrative is a form of confession, as she tells her story in her own words to us as readers. Her narration is also a kind of self-therapy, because Rachel's inability to express herself is her major character flaw, both symptom and cause of her neurosis. As Laurence said, "we must attempt to communicate, however imperfectly, if we are not to succumb to despair or madness" (*Long* 124–25). *A Jest of God* records Rachel's struggle to save her sanity and survive in a sometimes insane world.

Speech is the faculty that distinguishes human beings from other animals. Speech also distinguishes the living from the dead, "the unspeaking ones" (13) in the mortuary downstairs. In *A Jest of God*, silence is a sign of death, speech a proof of life. Rachel's silence is one of the signs of her moribund nature. Calla's canary Jacob, the silent songbird who dislikes hymns and love songs alike, is a symbol of the mute Rachel (47), for Rachel has yet to find her tongue. So Rachel's narrative is proof that she is still alive.

As Rachel relates her inner and outer experience, the narrative forms an exercise in psychoanalysis, for Rachel is in dire need of therapy. Hanging on to sanity by her fingernails, Rachel is obsessed with fear of madness. Isolated in her own solipsistic world, imprisoned within her skull, Rachel is verging on schizophrenia. Laurence employs narrative method to demonstrate Rachel's split personality by dividing internal and external dialogue. The actual dialogue that Rachel reports contrasts ironically with Rachel's interior monologues.

Laurence wants to help women find their own voice, to give her heroines "the gift of tongues" (26). But Rachel's voice is stifled in interior monologues. Her only real outcries are silent screams distinguished by emphatic italics: *"My God. How can I stand — "* (17), she shrieks silently.

Voices are crucial to Laurence's narrative method in *A Jest of God*, for Rachel shares Laurence's ear for language, for the spoken word. "Voice" may be the most often repeated word in the novel, appearing dozens of times. Rachel apprehends reality as voices, recalling the lonely childhood night sounds of train whistles — "the trainvoice that said *don't stay don't stay just don't ever stay — go and keep on going, never mind where.* The mourning and mockery of that voice, like blues. The only lonelier sound I ever heard was the voices of the loons on the spruce-edged lake up at Galloping Mountain. . . . People say *loon*, meaning mad. Crazy as a loon. They were mad, those bird voices" (167–68).

Voice is evidence of identity. Rachel apprehends herself as a voice: "I can hear my own voice, eagerly abject" (45), as if she were listening to someone else. She identifies other people as voices also: her mother's coven of bridge cronies are heard as "voices. Shrill, sedate, not clownish to their ears but only to mine, and of such unadmitted sadness I can scarcely listen and yet cannot stop listening" (98). "My mother's archaic simper voice" (90) is the one that echoes most resonantly in her mind. She even hears her mother's voice in her dreams, as well as her dead father, whom she apprehends only as a disembodied voice: "his voice — his voice — so I know he is lying there among them, lying in state, king over them. He can't fool me. He says run away Rachel run away run away." Then "My mother is singing in a falsetto voice, the stylish tremolo, the ladies' choir voice" (19). Even in her dreams, her mother's voice is false. But so is Rachel's, for she can only speak in artificial voices.

When Rachel does speak out loud, it is in borrowed voices — the "Peter-Rabbitish voice" (4) of a simpering schoolmarm or the "robot's mechanical voice" (48) of the dummy she thinks she is, or her sister "Stacey's voice, her exact words" (183). Rachel is truly a polyphonic narrator: as well-read a woman as her creator, Rachel also speaks in the numerous voices of famous literary authors, from the Bible, through Shakespeare, Donne and Marvell, to Wordsworth and Kipling, as we saw in the discussion of literary allusions. Most insidious of all, she hears in her own words "this echo of my mother's voice" (4), as she speaks in "Mother's voice, lilting and ladylike" (78), revealing how she has internalized her mother's life-denying attitudes: *"A woman's most precious possession.* My mother's archaic simper voice" (89–90) — creating a prison within her own skull that she cannot escape from until she exorcizes her mother tongue and discovers her own.

Of course Rachel does speak; she just doesn't say what she really thinks. The actual dialogue that Rachel records forms an ironic contrast with her inner thoughts: for example, she answers her mother's query, "That you, Rachel?" with "Yes," but she thinks sarcastically, "Who does she think it is — the Angel of Death?" (94). Perhaps Laurence is using Rachel's duplicity to demonstrate Canadian caution or the Manawakan hypocrisy that Rachel has internalized.

Rachel does not speak because she has no one to talk to — except herself. She panics when two teenage girls overhear her address her own reflection in a washroom mirror, because talking to yourself is a supposed sign of madness. But Rachel has no one else to talk to except herself — and a God she claims not to believe in. In the discussion of religion in themes, we saw how often Rachel addressed God, praying involuntarily, unconsciously prefacing her thoughts with "Oh God!"

Repressed, Rachel's real voice erupts in three significant scenes. Her true voice, long stifled in the crypt on Japonica Street, finally surfaces in cryptic cries in the Tabernacle of the Risen and Reborn, where "the gift of tongues" has been given to the congregation (26). Rachel is afraid that Calla will speak, but it is Rachel who finally finds her tongue: "Not Calla's voice. Mine. Oh my God. Mine. The voice of Rachel" (36).

The voice of Rachel is mourning for her lost children, like her Biblical namesake. But this birth proves abortive, for Rachel rejects it as an "alien voice" (48). The etymology of hysteria suggests sexual frustration, and this implication applies to Rachel's outburst, for her outcry is the voice of both her spirit and her body rising from its tomb of repression to demand love of God and love of man. It prefigures her next outcry in her first orgasm with Nick when the word is made flesh: " 'Nick — *Nick* — ' Only his name. Only, at this moment, his name. The only word" (148). After his breakthrough, Rachel is able to "speak from faith, not logic" and say, "If I had a child, I would like it to be yours," echoing her namesake's cry, *Give me my children"* (148). The third and last time the voice of Rachel will issue from the tomb where it has been buried deep in her psyche is when she learns that the fruit of her womb is not a child but a tumour: "My speaking voice, and then only that other voice, wordless and terrible, the voice of some woman mourning for her children" (181) — the voice of Rachel — "Rachel weeping for her children refused to be comforted for her children, because they *were* not" (Jeremiah 31.15).

Rachel's lover Nick Kazlik is a catalyst for communication. Although he deserts her and she loses their child, Nick bequeaths her an invaluable legacy: through his loving, he teaches her to speak. Significantly, many of their early conversations take place on the telephone, that modern umbilical cord, nurturing Rachel's infant voice. She finds that she can talk with Nick: "He's easy to listen to. Easy as well, it almost seems, to reply to" (70). She talks to him in her imagination, prefacing her thoughts with, *Listen, Nick — "*: "I talk to him, when he is not here, and tell him everything I can think of" (138). Finally Rachel learns to speak in fact as well as in fantasy.

The turning point of the novel occurs when Rachel's inner voice, printed in italics, is echoed by her outer voice, when she knocks on the door of death and demands, *"Let me come in.* 'Let me come in.' That was my voice?" (119). Once she has learned to speak, she can climb the stairs out of the tomb back to life.

Finally Rachel learns not merely how to speak but how to sing, when she recalls the Psalm, *"Make me to hear joy and gladness, that the bones which Thou hast broken may rejoice"* (201), as she sets out of the road of life with a song of freedom and affirmation of the future.

## STRUCTURES AND STRATEGIES

### Introduction: The Tender Trap

Margaret Laurence conveys Rachel Cameron's predicament to the reader in the first three chapters of *A Jest of God*. Rachel's situation involves three settings: home, school, and church. These settings involve her relationship with three types of people: adults, children, and angels. The individuals who are central to each of these settings are Rachel's mother, James Doherty, and Calla Mackie — as Hector Jonas will later be central to the mortuary and the theme of death. Laurence devotes one chapter to each of these settings, for each is central to one of the novel's central types of love — sexual, maternal, and spiritual. Rachel is frustrated sexually, maternally, and spiritually to the point of explosion, and we will witness an outburst in each area.

### Home: Playing Guilt Like a Violin

At home, Rachel is the virtual prisoner of her hypochondriac mother, who entraps Rachel in a cocoon of perpetual childhood. She imprisons her in the same house over the mortuary where Rachel grew up, because Mrs. Cameron cannot abide the thought of moving. She says to Rachel, "it is your life, isn't it?" (78), but she does not really mean it. On the contrary, she seems to want to control Rachel completely. Laurence shows this symbolically when May Cameron circles Rachel's wrist with a mauve-veined, sapphire-ringed hand like a manacle (101), making Rachel feel "as though a leather thong had lassoed my temples" (81).

Mrs. Cameron plays polite power games: as Rachel observes, "Her weapons are invisible" (40). Rachel recalls that her mother never spanked her, but always chastised her "more in sorrow than anger" (28) — like the ghost of Hamlet's father, even using religion to strengthen her power play: "She used to tell me over and over how my misdemeanours wounded her. They also hurt Jesus, as I recollect. Well, poor Jesus. No doubt He weathered it better than I did" (78).

Mrs. Cameron also plays the martyr to perfection: the first time

Rachel goes out with Nick, her mother threatens to wash the blankets! As Margaret Atwood says, Rachel's mother "plays guilt like a violin" (214), using her weak heart as a way of controlling her daughter, because "Her heart is very tricky and could vanquish her at any moment" (14). Rachel is even afraid to go out, in case her mother should have a heart attack in her absence: "All my fault" (66). If she died, her death would be on Rachel's head, leaving her "forever in the wrong" (73), burdened with perpetual guilt. So the only excursions Rachel is allowed are guilt trips. Rachel's most frequent comment is, "I'm sorry, Mother" (66), as she apologizes her life away.

The problem of communication is raised in this first relationship, for May Cameron, like the delicate dowagers of her generation, will never say what she means. Rachel complains, "If only once she'd say what she means, and we could have it out. But she won't" (67). "Circumlocution is necessary for mother" (58), Rachel observes, "We could pace this treadmill indefinitely" (67), but she can not break these bonds. Consequently, Rachel is also forced into deception: "It isn't that I want to lie to her. But she invites it, even demands it. Whoever said the truth shall make you free never knew this kind of house" (100).

Rachel refuses two invitations in the first few pages of the novel because it is her mother's bridge night, and she has to wait on the "coven" of old ladies as an unpaid maid. Rachel realizes, "I could have gone to Willard's for dinner. I could have gone with Calla," but "I don't begrudge it to her, this one evening of bridge with the only three long long friends. How could I? No one decent would" (15). But Rachel is frustrated by her mother's power plays to the point of exploding: she screams in her invisible voice, *My God. How can I stand —* " (17). Not until she becomes involved with Nick Kazlik will she break free from her mother's tender trap.

Rachel has inherited many of her repressive attitudes from her mother, who worships the old-fashioned small-town gods of Propriety and Decorum. She loathes scenes, considers childbirth out of wedlock a "heartbreak" (58), and hates to see people (like old Tom Gillanders) make fools of themselves.

Trapped by her mother in a perpetual childhood, Rachel is denied adult social and sexual relationships. The first chapter explodes with Rachel's masturbation fantasy of the "shadow prince." But she feels guilty about her sexuality: "I didn't. I didn't. It was only to be able to sleep. The shadow prince. Am I unbalanced? Or only laughable? That's worse, much worse" (19).

## School: Teacher's Pet

Rachel's maternal instincts are just as frustrated as her sexual instincts. She envies her married sister Stacey her four children: "They think they are making a shelter for their children, but actually it is the children who are making a shelter for them" (50). A spinster schoolteacher with no children of her own, Rachel grows attached to her pupils, calling them her children, although she knows she should not: "I have to gather my children in. I must stop referring to them as my children" (2).

When Nick asks how she likes teaching, Rachel explains her distress: "There's nothing lasting. They move on, and that's that. It's such a brief thing. I know them only for a year, and then I see them changing but I don't know them any more" (108). Her students change, but Rachel remains: "They seem like a different race, a separate species, all those generations of children" (1).

Each year, Rachel becomes emotionally attached to one child. This year her teacher's pet is James Doherty, creator of *"splendid"* spaceships. Acknowledging that "I care about James" (25), Rachel realizes she must conceal her favouritism, lest they "torment me. . . . But James would be cruel too" (6).

James's absenteeism after tonsillitis provokes a crisis. Willard Siddley, the sadistic school principal, orders Rachel to send James to his office to be strapped, so Rachel feels guilty for betraying James (25). When she interviews James's mother, Grace Doherty, about James's absence, she feels jealous because she cannot, unlike his mother, touch him with tenderness. When James conceals his paper from her, she assumes that his is hiding "A caricature? An unendurable portrait?" of her. His stubborn refusal to reveal his paper catapults her into hostile fury: "He hates me. I am the enemy" (52). Rachel's frustrated maternal instinct erupts in automatic violence, and she strikes him across the face with her ruler, making his nose bleed. His pathetic paper reveals "No obscene caricatures. Only — two sums completed, out of ten, and those two done incorrectly" (53). She wants to say, *"James — I'm sorry"* (53), but she is afraid to admit her vulnerability. She fears that she has alienated him forever and that in future years he will remember only her outburst of violence.

## Church: Propriety and Decorum

Religion is the third area where Rachel is repressed. Although Rachel believes that God is dead, she attends Church because her mother said, "I don't think it would be very nice, not to go. I don't think it would look very good" (39). Emphasis on propriety is paramount in church, and so that is where Rachel's repression is rampant. Fortunately, the Presbyterian church, with its decorous hymns and safe sermon, poses little threat: "If the Reverend MacElfrish should suddenly lose his mind and speak of God with anguish or joy, or out of some need should pray with fierce humility as though God had to be there, Mother would be shocked to the core. Luckily, it will never happen" (41).

No such security exists at The Tabernacle of the Risen and Reborn, however, where the sermon and hymns are unabashedly passionate and the congregation has been vouchsafed the "gift of tongues" (26). Rachel is hideously embarrassed by such fervent expressions of faith. Amid their "alien voices," her repressed religious instincts erupt in an outburst of hysteria during "that indefensible moment, trapped in my own alien voice, and the eyes all around have swollen to giants' eyes" (48). Her horror is exacerbated by Calla's kiss of comfort: "as though unpremeditated, she kisses my face and swiftly afterwards my mouth" (38). Rachel associates her religious outcry to God with Calla's lesbian pass, and she runs away from both as fast as she can: "run away Rachel run away run away" (19).

The grand finale of the introductory three chapters of the novel outlining Rachel's sexual, maternal, and religious repression is Rachel's erotic fantasy of a Roman orgy at the ancient Egyptian court of Queen Cleopatra (59). This vivid scenario provides a perfect prelude to Rachel's romance with Nick Kazlik.

## Development

The stereotypical spinster schoolteacher, Rachel is sexually repressed to the point of hysteria. A thirty-four-year-old arrested adolescent, she feels the burden of her own virginity like "an oxen yoke" (92) that she wants to throw off. Rachel realizes, "Women like me are an anachronism. We don't exist any more. And yet I look in the mirror and see I'm there. I'm a fact of sorts, a fantasy of sorts. My blood

94

runs in actual veins, which is as much of a surprise to me as to anyone" (117). Certainly Rachel is ready for romance.

## Catalyst: Summer Romance

Summer is in full bloom when Rachel first meets Nick during his visit home. Nick's greeting interrupts her inner reverie (62), but he will teach her to live in the real world, not just in the "deep theatre" (90) of her own imagination. Nick is the catalyst for Rachel's long overdue development. Rachel begins to develop four crucial qualities for survival: a sense of independence, a sense of humour and the ability to communicate and to love. Let us follow Rachel's development, as Laurence depicts it gradually, naturally, and skilfully.

First, Rachel begins to demonstrate a healthy adult independence from her tyrannical mother, refusing to play the power game when Mrs. Cameron threatens to wash the blankets if Rachel goes out, endangering her weak heart. Rachel replies to her mother's astonishment, "All right. Wash them if you like. I can't stop you, can I?" (68). For the moment she thinks, "I don't care. I don't give a damn. I'll care later. Not right now" (68). She even, heaven forbid, leaves her mother's bridge party to see Nick: when her mother protests, Rachel forces herself not to capitulate: *"I won't go, then* — I find the words are there already in my throat, and yet I force them back. This newfound ruthlessness exhilarates me. I won't turn back. If I do, I'm done for" (101). Rachel is growing up at last. Ironically, by freeing herself from her mother's death grip, Rachel learns to view her mother as vulnerable (114) and to care for her with compassion. So she learns to love her mother rather than fear her.

Equally important, under the tutelage of the arch-mocker Nick, Rachel also develops a sense of humour. When her mother asks how Nick Kazlik, the milkman's son, managed to become a high school teacher, Rachel replies, "Some miracle, I suppose. Divine intervention, maybe" (65). When her mother calls out, "That you, Rachel?" she thinks, "Who does she think it is — the Angel of Death?" (94). Gradually Rachel learns to laugh, and eventually she even gets the joke.

More important, Rachel learns from Nick to express herself, to communicate with another human being. First she thinks, "He's easy to listen to. Easy as well, it almost seems, to reply to" (70). Later she thinks, "He's easy to laugh with," and "I feel as though I might talk to him and he would know what I meant" (107). Nick becomes her imaginary confidant, as she prefaces her innermost thoughts with an unspoken *"Listen, Nick — "*: "I talk to him, when he is not here, and tell him everything I can think of, everything that has ever happened, and how I feel and for a while it seems to me that I am completely known to him" (138). When Rachel begins to speak in Nick's idiom, saying, "You know?" we know who her speech instructor is: "I catch in my own voice something of Nick's — *You know?* I didn't mean to copy. But something of him inhabits me yet" (195).

Most important, Rachel learns to love, as the "milkman's son" awakens the "undertaker's daughter" (67), a modern Sleeping Beauty on the banks of the Wachakwa River. With his first kiss, Nick unleashes desires that have surfaced only in her private fantasies: "Oh my God. Now I really do want him. Now I would do anything" (72). Nick's kiss is an effective antidote to Calla's, for Calla's lesbian overture threatened Rachel: "Could a person be Calla's way, without knowing it, only it might be obvious to a man" (83).

Their first lovemaking in the Wachakwa River Valley is not totally satisfactory since it is *"the first time"* for Rachel (92). Still, she feels a profound sense of peace, of pride (91). Later she thinks, "I'm fantastically happy. He did want me. And I wasn't afraid. I think that when he is with me, I don't feel any fear. Or hardly any. Soon I won't feel any at all" (94). And the next time, in Nick's home, she is unafraid: "See — I have changed" (103); "I'm not afraid when I am with him" (131). Most important, she learns to love: "Nick — listen — I love you" (114). Now that she can love emotionally, she can also love physically. The third and last time they make love, in their "summer house," their lovemaking is entirely satisfying to both of them: "Nothing is complicated. He inhabits whatever core of me there is. I can move outward to him, knowing he wants what I am, and I can receive him, whatever he is, whatever. And then this tender cruelty, always known to him but never before to me, the unmattering of what either of us is" (147). For the first time, Rachel sheds her crippling self-consciousness and learns to express herself sexually, even achieving the orgasm that her earlier violent outbursts were imitating. Learning that someone can inhabit her — a man or a baby — she learns to live in her own body at last, no longer wearing her hands "like empty gloves" (8).

Rachel's most pressing need is not just for sexual love, but maternal love. Even more than a lover, she wants a child. When she says to Nick, the last time they make love, "If I had a child, I would like it to be yours," Nick realizes the depths of her desperation. He replies, "I'm not God. I can't solve anything" (148). Realizing that he, unlike God with the biblical Rachel, cannot fulfil her needs, Nick withdraws. His method of rejection is subtle: showing her a faded snapshot of a boy, Nick lets Rachel think it is his own. After he mysteriously disappears, Rachel learns from his parents that he is unmarried. The snapshot may have been himself as a boy or even his phantom twin. Rachel realizes, "He had his own demons and webs. Mine brushed across him for an instant, and he saw them and had to draw away, knowing that what I wanted from him was too much" (189).

Nick's mysterious disappearance forces Rachel to face reality for the first time: "The layers of dream are so many, so many false membranes grown around the mind, that I don't even know they are there until some knifing reality cuts through, and I see the sight of my other eyes for what it has been, distorted, bizarre, grotesque, unbearably a joke if viewed from the outside" (150–51). Rachel tries to be realistic about their romance: "I don't believe it was completely nothing, for him. Do I deceive myself? More than likely. I don't know — that's the thing. I never knew him very well. We were not well acquainted. We talked sometimes, and I tried to hear what he was saying, but I'm not certain I did hear. I may have heard only guarded echoes of his voice. He never spoke of his real life, the one he leads away from here" (154). But then neither did she.

Symbolically, their summer romance fades in the fall, and Rachel returns to reality as school commences in September and she ushers a new group of children into her classroom: "They troop in, two by two, all the young animals into my Ark" (154). She realizes that her initiation into reality has also finished something: "I wonder who will be the one or ones, as it was James last year? All at once I know there will be no one like that, not now, not any more. This unwanted revelation fills me with the sense of an ending" (155).

### Crisis: Putative Pregnancy

Nick is not the only catalytic agent in Rachel's life. A putative pregnancy forces her to develop because she cannot be a mother while she is still a child. For a woman in the small prairie town of Manawaka in the mid-sixties, bearing a child out of wedlock, especially for a schoolteacher, the epitome of respectability, is unthinkable. Laurence makes this clear through the figure of Cassie Stewart who gives birth to twins. Mrs. Cameron voices the shocked disapproval of the community, calling the birth a "heartbreak" (58).

The pregnancy forces Rachel to make the greatest decision of her life, as she endures an agonizing conflict: "There are three worlds and I'm in the middle one, and this seems now to be a weak area between millstones" (94). Caught in a dilemma, she debates: "It can't be borne," and "It can't be ended, either" (169). The idea of bearing a child seems a miracle to Rachel, the miracle of life: "I could bear a living creature. It would be possible" (163). But she realizes, "I can't bear it. I have to get rid of it" (163), because social pressure makes it impossible: "Left to myself, would I destroy this only one? I can't bear it, that's all. It isn't to be borne. I can't face it. I can't face them" (165). Like her mother, she thinks, *"What will become of me?"* (160). Her repeated refrain, "It can't be borne" (169), has a nice ambiguity.

Rachel's insoluble dilemma drives her to the verge of suicide. Unable to abort the child and unable to face people's opprobrium, she determines to take her own life, rather than give life to another creature. Suicidal, she settles down in the bathroom late at night with fatal legacies from both parents — fourteen of her mother's sleeping pills (one for each year in Manawaka *and* for Jacob's labour for his Rachel) and a bottle of her father's whiskey. Realizing, *"They will all go on in some how, all of them, but I will be dead as stone and it will be too late then to change my mind"* (170), she impulsively tosses the pills onto the mortuary lawn, where they belong.

Desperate, she falls on her knees and prays — "Only out of need. Not faith, or belief" — to the "Last resort": *"Help me."* Unlike Jonah, Rachel does not receive a response: "If You have a voice, it is not comprehensible to me. No omens. No burning bush, no pillar of sand by day or pillar of flame by night" (171). She finally realizes she is alone: "There isn't anyone. I'm on my own. I never knew before what that would be like. It means no one. Just that. Just — myself" (165). Realizing that it is up to her, she rejects death for the sake of the child she believes is *"[l]odged"* (173) within her "bonehouse" (182). Instead, she elects life for herself and her offspring: "Look — it's my child, mine. And so I will have it. I will have it because I want it and because I cannot do anything else" (171). As a result of choosing to bear a child, with all the trials that must involve for a single woman, Rachel develops into an independent, responsible adult. She even liberates herself from her chains of guilt when her mother plays her trump card, a weak heart: "My mother's tricky heart will just have to take its own chances" (176), Rachel decides.

## Climax: God's Jest

Here comes the punch line, the jest of God of the title: Rachel is not gestating life but death. Doctor Raven, well named for a harbinger of death, sends her plummeting to purgatory when he discovers that she is incubating not an embryo but a tumour. "How can non-life be a growth?" she questions. *"Oh my God. I didn't bargain for this. Not this"* (180). Surgery proves that "Doctor Raven was right, dead right" (182): the growth was a deadly, not a living one. Stretched out on a metal table like the one in Hector's mortuary, with her feet strapped in the stirrups to ride birth, Rachel delivers death.

This is the ultimate jest of God, for the decision to bear the child that cost Rachel so much seems all for nothing: "Only now do I recall the long discussions with myself. *What will I do? Where will I go?* The decision, finally. It cost me something, that decision, you know?" (181). However, the tumour is not *malignant* but *benign* (180) — like God Himself — for Rachel does give birth, not to an infant but to a new adult self. She has also gained a child, for she realizes, "I am the mother now" (196) of her "elderly child" (201).

## Conclusion: Reluctant Jester

God has the last laugh, but Rachel finally gets the joke. She has always been afraid of being foolish: "I'm not a fool" (46), she insisted, and "I can't bear watching people make fools of themselves" (27). "If I believed, I would have to detest God for the brutal joker He would be if He existed" (42). Saint Paul taught, *"If any man among you thinketh himself to be wise, let him become a fool, that he may be wise"* (135). Rachel has taken a long time to develop a spiritual sense of humour: embarrassed by her sexual awkwardness with Nick, she said, "All right, God — go ahead and laugh, and I'll laugh with you, but not quite yet for a while" (115). Finally she gets the joke: "All that. And this at the end of it. I was always afraid that I might become a fool. Yet I could almost smile with some grotesque lightheadedness at that fool of a fear, that poor fear of fools, now that I really am one" (181). Rachel realizes, "What is so terrible about fools? I should be honoured to be of that company" (198). Becoming a fool, she can now be wise — wise enough to pity the Joker Himself: "God's mercy on reluctant jesters. God's grace on fools. God's pity on God" (202).

Like Jonah and Job, Rachel has survived her suffering and learned joy, as she recalls the words of the Psalm: *"Make me to hear joy and gladness, that the bones which Thou hast broken may rejoice"* (201). She wonders, "I do not know how many bones need be broken before I can walk. And I do not know, either, how many need not have been broken at all" (201).


### Denouement: Last Laugh

Rachel makes her farewells — to Willard, Calla, and Hector. Saying goodbye to Willard, Rachel realizes that she need never have feared him. Recognizing Willard's own insecurity, Rachel spares his feelings, concealing how much she has disliked his school. Calla empathizes with Rachel's false pregnancy, saying, "I'm sorry that things weren't different for you" (197) and reassures her, "heavens, child, [being a fool] is the least of your worries" (198). Realizing "the truth is that she loves me" (198), Rachel acknowledges Calla's love, saying, "I'm sorry things weren't different for you. I mean that I wasn't different" (198). When Hector shows Rachel his new sign, *"Japonica Chapel"* in crimson neon letters, Rachel's response is philosophical: "It's a change, Hector. It's — evolution" (201), because it is time for Rachel too to make a change. The final irony occurs when Hector reveals the rumour that Rachel's trip to the city of Winnipeg for surgery was really to secure an illegal abortion or to repair the damage of a self-induced abortion. Rachel is able to feel some amusement, thinking, "The ironies go on" (200), but this final irony shows how right she is to leave Manawaka with its small-town mentality.

The novel concludes with embarkation, as Rachel sets out on the road of life with her "elderly child" (201). Finally allowing the winds of fate to waft her, she sets off for her *"golden city"* (1) of Vancouver, en route to reunion with her sister Stacey in a new spirit of freedom:

Where I'm going, anything may happen. Nothing may happen. Maybe I will marry a middle-aged widower, or a longshoreman, or a cattle-hoof-trimmer, or a barrister or a thief. And have my children in time. Or maybe not. Most of the chances are against it. But not, I think, quite all. What will happen? What will happen. It may be that my children will always be temporary, never to be held. But so are everyone's. . . . The wind will bear me, and I will drift and settle, and drift and settle. Anything may happen, where I'm going. (201)

Finally, Rachel combines optimism with realism in an affirmative vision of the future.

# Works Cited

Atwood, Margaret. "Face to Face." *Maclean's* May 1974: 38+. Rpt. in New 33–40.
    Includes biographical information and comments by Laurence.
_____. Afterword. *A Jest of God*. By Margaret Laurence. New Canadian Library. Toronto: McClelland, 1988. 211–15.
    Provides a feminist perspective and points out the relevance of the novel for contemporary women.
Bailey, Nancy. "Margaret Laurence, Carl Jung and the Manawaka Woman." *Studies in Canadian Literature* 2 (1977): 306–21.
    Links the growth in awareness of Laurence's heroines to the theories of Carl Jung.
Blewett, David. "The Unity of the Manawaka Cycle." *Journal of Canadian Studies* 13.3 (1978): 31–39.
    Fascinating discussion of the four Manawaka novels as unified, each as a part of a whole vision of the human condition.
Boone, Laurel. "Rachel's Benign Growth." *Studies in Canadian Literature* 3 (1978): 277–81.
    Sees Rachel's tumour as symbolic of "nonlife" rather than a blatant symbol of death.
Bowering, George. "That Fool of a Fear: Notes on *A Jest of God*." *Canadian Literature* 50 (1971): 41–56. Rpt. in Woodcock 210–26.
    An important analysis of form and language in the novel.
Brydon, Diana. "Silence, Voice and the Mirror: Margaret Laurence and Women." Gunnars 183–205.
    Focuses on the interaction of the novels and their feminist audience.
Cameron, Donald. "Margaret Laurence: The Black Celt Speaks of Freedom." *Conversations with Canadian Novelists – 1*. Toronto: Macmillan, 1973. 96–115.
    An important interview that includes discussion of Laurence's childhood on the prairies, the theme of isolation, the autobiographical aspect of her fiction, and her sense of history, the Bible, and her Presbyterian heritage.
Djwa, Sandra. "False Gods and the True Covenant: Thematic Continuity between Margaret Laurence and Sinclair Ross." *Journal of Canadian Fiction* 1 (1972): 43–50. Rpt. in New 66–84.

A discussion of Ross's *As for Me and My House* and Laurence's novels in terms of their "sense of the ironic discrepancy between the spirit and the letter of the religious dispensation."

Forman, Denyse, and Uma Parameswaran. "Echoes and Refrains in the Canadian Novels of Margaret Laurence." *Centennial Review* 16 (1972): 233–53. Rpt. in New 85–100.

Excellent discussion of the characters, themes, and techniques running through *The Fire-Dwellers*, *The Stone Angel*, and *A Jest of God*.

Fulford, Robert. "A Painful Life in a Prairie Town." Rev. of *A Jest of God*, by Margaret Laurence. *Toronto Daily Star* 30 Sept. 1966: 21.

Views book as "painful" in many ways, but as "a minor triumph."

Fulton, Keith Louise. "Feminism and Humanism: Margaret Laurence and the 'Crisis of the Imagination.'" Gunnars 99–120.

Provides a good discussion of Laurence's feminism.

Gibson, Graeme. "Margaret Laurence, An Interview." *Eleven Canadian Novelists*. Toronto: Anansi, 1973. 181–208.

Includes Laurence's views on the nature of the novel, the effect of film on writers, the writer's role in society, and the position of the woman writer.

Gom, Leona. "Margaret Laurence and the First Person." *Dalhousie Review* 55 (1975): 235–51.

Analyzes Laurence's use of the first person, the distinction between reliable and unreliable narrators in the Manawaka novels, and her use of mirror images.

——. "Laurence and the Use of Memory." *Canadian Literature* 71 (1976): 48–58.

Analyzes the use of subjective time as memory in the Manawaka novels.

Gunnars, Kristjana, ed. *Crossing the River: Essays in Honour of Margaret Laurence*. Winnipeg: Turnstone, 1988.

Hall, Joan Joffe. "Prison of the Self." Rev. of *A Jest of God*, by Margaret Laurence. *Saturday Review* 27 Aug. 1966: 29.

Praises the authenticity of Rachel's voice and the novel's detail, but feels that the first-person narration "accentuates the novel's limitations."

Harlow, Robert. "Lack of Distance." Rev. of *A Jest of God*, by Margaret Laurence. *Canadian Literature* 31 (1967): 71+. Rpt. in New 189–91.

An unfavourable, "chauvinist response" to the novel.

Hughes, Kenneth James. "Politics and *A Jest of God*." *Journal of Canadian Studies* 13.3 (1978): 40–54.

Political approach.

*Journal of Canadian Fiction* 27 (1980).

Special issue on "The Work of Margaret Laurence."

*Journal of Canadian Studies* 13.3 (1978).

Special issue on Laurence.

Kearns, Judy. "Rachel and Social Determinism: A Feminist Reading of *A Jest of*

God." *Journal of Canadian Fiction* 27 (1980): 101–23.

Discusses Rachel's internalizing of conventional attitudes and the techniques used to provide distance from the narrator's internalized values.

Killam, G.D. Introduction. *A Jest of God.* By Margaret Laurence. New Canadian Library 111. Toronto: McClelland, 1974. N. pag.

Sees central theme as the need to communicate.

Kroetsch, Robert. "A Conversation with Margaret Laurence." *Creation.* Ed. Robert Kroetsch. Toronto: new, 1970. 53–63.

Includes Kroetsch's and Laurence's ideas of writing, of symbol and character, and of their sense of the West.

Laurence, Margaret, ed. and trans. *A Tree for Poverty: Somali Poetry and Prose.* Nairobi: Eagle, 1954. Translation.

_____ . *This Side Jordan.* Toronto: McClelland, 1960. Novel.

_____ . *The Tomorrow-Tamer.* Toronto: McClelland, 1963. Stories.

_____ . *The Prophet's Camel Bell.* Toronto: McClelland, 1963. Essays.

_____ . *The Stone Angel.* Toronto: McClelland, 1964. Novel.

_____ . *A Jest of God.* Toronto: McClelland, 1966. Novel.

_____ . *Long Drums and Cannons: Nigerian Dramatists and Novelists 1952–1966.* London: Macmillan, 1968. Criticism.

_____ . *The Fire-Dwellers.* Toronto: McClelland, 1969. Novel.

_____ . "Ten Years' Sentences." *Canadian Literature* 41 (1969): 10–16. Rpt. in New 17–23.

_____ . *A Bird in the House: Stories.* Toronto: McClelland, 1970. Stories.

_____ . "A Place to Stand on (1970)." Woodcock 15–19. Essay.

_____ . "Sources." *Mosaic* 3.3 (1970): 80–84. Rpt. in New 12–16.

_____ . *Jason's Quest.* Toronto: McClelland, 1970. Children's fiction.

_____ . "Time and the Narrative Voice." *The Narrative Voice.* Ed. John Metcalf. Toronto: McGraw, 1972. 126–30. Rpt. in New 156–60.

_____ . *The Diviners.* Toronto: McClelland, 1974. Novel.

_____ . *Heart of a Stranger.* Toronto: McClelland, 1976. Essays.

_____ . "Ivory Towers or Grassroots?: The Novelist as Socio-Political Being." *A Political Art: Essays and Images in Honour of George Woodcock.* Ed. William H. New. Vancouver: U of British Columbia P, 1978. 15–25. Essay.

_____ . *Six Darn Cows.* Toronto: Lorimer, 1979. Children's fiction.

_____ . *The Olden Days Coat.* Toronto: McClelland, 1979. Children's fiction.

_____ . *The Christmas Birthday Story.* Toronto: McClelland, 1980. Children's fiction.

_____ . "Gadgetry or Growing: Form and Voice in the Novel." *Journal of Canadian Fiction* 27 (1980): 54–62. Rpt. in Woodcock 80–89. Essay.

McCourt, Edward A. *The Canadian West in Fiction.* Rev. ed. Toronto: Ryerson, 1970.

Discusses Manawaka as the background of Laurence's fiction.

McLay, C.M. "Every Man is an Island: Isolation in *A Jest of God.*" *Canadian*

*Literature* 50 (1971): 57–68. Rpt. in New 177–88.

    Traces the theme of isolation in the novel.

Morley, Patricia. *Margaret Laurence.* Twayne's World Authors 591. Boston: Twayne, 1981.

    General overview of Laurence's life and works.

Moss, John. *Sex and Violence in the Canadian Novel: The Ancestral Present.* Toronto: McClelland, 1977.

    Argues that "sexual behaviour in Laurence's women is inseparable from their total experience of themselves."

New, William H., ed. *Margaret Laurence.* Critical Views on Canadian Writers. Toronto: McGraw, 1977.

    Includes reviews, critical articles, and articles by Laurence.

Rosengarten, H.J. "Inescapable Bonds." *Canadian Literature* 35 (1968): 99–100. Rpt. in New 192–93.

    A response to Harlow's review.

Stevenson, Warren. "The Myth of Demeter and Persephone in *A Jest of God.*" *Studies in Canadian Literature* 1 (1976): 120–23.

    Examines the interaction of Rachel and her mother in terms of the myth of Demeter and Persephone.

Thomas, Clara. *Margaret Laurence.* Canadian Writers 3. Toronto: McClelland, 1969.

    General introduction which includes a chapter on *A Jest of God.*

———. *The Manawaka World of Margaret Laurence.* New Canadian Library 131. Toronto: McClelland, 1976.

    Includes biographical information, analyses of the works, and discussions of Laurence's concern with the past, individual and cultural, and with place.

———. "The Novels of Margaret Laurence." *Studies in the Novel* 4.2 (1972): 152–64. Rpt. in New 55–65.

    Detailed study of Laurence's handling of voice, time, and the journey motif in three novels.

Van Herk, Aritha. "The Eulalias of Spinsters and Undertakers." Gunnars 133–45.

    A feminist reading which unites Rachel's religious glossalalia with her orgasmic eulalia.

Warwick, Susan J. "A Laurence Log." *Journal of Canadian Studies* 13.3 (1978): 75–83.

    Includes a chronological listing of events in Laurence's life as a writer to 1978 and a bibliography of secondary books, articles, and theses.

———. "Margaret Laurence: An Annotated Bibliography." *The Annotated Bibliography of Canada's Major Authors.* Ed. Robert Lecker and Jack David. Vol. 1. Downsview, ON: ECW, 1979. 47–101.

Woodcock, George, ed. *A Place to Stand On: Essays by and about Margaret Laurence.* WCLD 4. Edmonton: NeWest, 1983.

# Index

Date Due